SUPER
MEMORY

SUPER MEMORY

A QUICK-ACTION PROGRAMME FOR MEMORY IMPROVEMENT

DOUGLAS J. HERRMANN

BLANDFORD

To Donna, Amanda, and Zachary

A BLANDFORD BOOK

First published in the UK by Blandford in 1995
A Cassell Imprint
Cassell Plc, Wellington House
125 Strand, London WC2R 0BB

Reprinted 1996, 1997, 1999

**British Library Cataloguing-in-Publication
Data**
A catalogue entry for this title is available from
the British Library.

ISBN 0–7137–2507–9

Printed and bound in Great Britain by
Biddles Ltd, Guildford and King's Lynn

CONTENTS

Answers you know but can't recall . . . Names of authors
. . . Information on an unfamiliar topic raised in conversa-
tion . . . Current events . . . Important dates in time . . .
Geographical locations and terrain . . . Grammatical usage
. . . Historical facts . . . Information you've read . . . Jokes
and anecdotes . . . Foreign languages . . . Foreign
phrases for travel . . . Content of lectures and meetings . . .
Lyrics of songs . . . Systems for solving math problems . . .
Tunes . . . Phone numbers, other numbers . . . Poetry . . .
Prose . . . Game rules . . . Lines for a role in a play . . .
Speeches . . . Spelling . . . Trivia . . . Vocabulary . . .
Songwriters and singers

Personal routine duties . . . Birthdays . . . Cards already played in a game . . . What you were saying when interrupted . . . Details of past conversations . . . Dates of future events . . . Verbal instructions for a procedure . . . Directions for a travel route . . . Childhood events . . . Events important to you . . . Details of parties, vacations, and the like . . . Familiar faces . . . Misplaced files . . . Recalling a first meeting . . . Diet details . . . Ingredients used in preparing a recipe . . . Money or objects you lend . . . Missing keys . . . Misplaced object . . . Long-lost objects . . . Your parked car's location . . . Long statements, questions, or requests . . . Messages received when you're sleepy . . . Names of people introduced to you . . . Names of old acquaintances . . . Names of people in a receiving line . . . What food and drinks you have served to whom at a social occasion . . . Photos: time, place, subjects, and photographer . . . Places visited on a trip . . . Views you expressed on an issue . . . Contents of personal correspondence . . . What you said to whom

Routine tasks before leaving the house . . . A new routine to follow . . . Appointments and meetings . . . Cards and gifts to be sent . . . Taking your change after a purchase . . . Necessary chores . . . Unpleasant tasks . . . Turning off the range or oven . . . Correspondence due . . . Low-priority deadlines . . . Serving all the dishes you prepared for a meal . . . Buttons, zippers, and accessories . . . Errands . . . What you're looking for in a room . . . Information given in a hectic situation . . . Taking your keys with you . . . Maintenance of your car and household appliances . . . Medication as scheduled . . . Packing essentials for a trip . . . Taking what you brought (and bought) back home . . . Paying your bills on time . . . Making necessary phone calls . . . Returning library books . . . Resetting clocks for seasonal time changes . . . New ideas with no time to make notes . . . Important thoughts during sleep time . . . Starting on time . . . Turning off lights when you leave a room . . . Getting up on time

PREFACE

I first got interested in memory when I was a student at the U.S. Naval Academy in Annapolis. One day I happened to see an ad for a mail-order memory course by a man named Bruno Furst. The ad said the course was quick, easy, and it would improve my memory in hundreds of ways. It cost $15 for all 15 lessons.

The naval academy was pretty tough and I wanted to get the best grades I could with the least amount of effort, so I decided to give Bruno Furst a shot. The only problem was, I didn't *have* $15.

Luckily, the ad offered a deal—you could try the course for ten days free, and if you weren't completely satisfied, you could return it without having to pay a dime. I figured that I'd order the course, study the whole thing in ten days, and send it back.

When the course arrived in the mail, I went through it in three or four days. It was pretty basic stuff. I didn't learn much, but I did learn a few things, and something kept me from wanting to send it back by the end of the trial period.

I figured that Bruno Furst would just forget about the $15 and that would be the end of it. Well, Bruno Furst apparently never forgot *anything*. One day a note arrived in the mail that simply said, "Remember, it's important for people to know you can be faithful to your obligations. See Lesson 7, paragraph 2." Bruno Furst was on to me.

The next day another note arrived with a wise saying on it, and another one came every day after that.

Well, my roommates just ate it up. They put the notes on bulletin boards all over the campus, and my memory became the butt of many jokes. Humiliated, I finally scrounged around for the money and wrote out a check to Bruno Furst.

That was the first time I really noticed the field of memory improvement, and I've pretty much devoted my career to it ever since. Think of it: If you want, you can open your eyes, look at an image for a fraction of a second, and remember it for the rest of your life. The human memory is such a marvelous machine! Yet it can still fail with startling regularity. This is why I find the field so fascinating.

Despite the fact that my wife and daughter like to joke about my terrible memory, I *have* learned a thing or two about the human memory since my naval academy days, and I'm looking forward to sharing them with you. But listen—no money back guarantees. Okay?

ACKNOWLEDGMENTS

Several people have influenced and shaped my thinking about memory improvement over the years. I am indebted to them for their ideas and the help they gave me.

John McLaughlin encouraged my interest in the subject, Dick Atkinson stimulated me to make it an object of research, Jack Carroll helped me appreciate how memory depends on language and thought, Dick Neisser convinced me that memory research should address situations in everyday life, and Herman Buschke taught me to pay attention to the subtleties of memory processing.

My decision to write this book was made while on sabbatical at the Applied Psychology Unit in Cambridge, England, during 1982–1983.

A second sabbatical at the University of Manchester in England, supported by their Simon Fellowship, provided the opportunity to investigate memory improvement and write much of this book.

I am especially appreciative of Jim Reason's efforts to bring me to Manchester for the year and for many useful discussions with him, Pat Rabbitt, and Graham Hitch about the effects of memory training.

Many people have helped in the creation of this book.

I am grateful to the many students who did such excellent work on projects that gave me new insights on memory improvement.

Several of the people who read drafts of this book gave me valuable advice about the content and style; among them: Donna Herrmann, Steve Andrzejewski, Wendy Weber, John McLaughlin, Roger Chaffin, and Jonathan Schooler.

I thank Michael Gervasio and Edward Walters for clarifying the writing.

And I am indebted to Nancy Ernst, Nancy Hardy, and Sheila Vincent for helping with a variety of activities concerned with putting the book together or with other activities that freed the time I needed to devote to this project. I am especially grateful to Michael Gruneberg and Margaret Matlin for encouraging me to continue working on this book at times when I needed encouragement.

In conclusion, I especially thank Dan Gutman for rewriting much of my last draft. He has made the book more readable and more enjoyable. Much of the humor and sparkle found here are Dan's. Also, many parts of this book are much clearer because Dan (who has done graduate work in cognitive psychology) possesses a special understanding of psychological issues. In certain cases Dan even suggested some ways I had not included to improve memory for particular tasks. I feel very fortunate to have had his help.

INTRODUCTION: A NEW VIEW ON MEMORY

Do you find that you can recall every word of lyrics to songs you heard when you were 13, but you can't remember where you left your house keys five minutes ago?

Do you inexplicably know the lifetime batting average of every member of the Baseball Hall of Fame, even though you never made any effort to learn them?

When you go to the movies, do you find that you become confused because you can't remember who is in love with whom, who killed whom, or which characters are related to each other?

Do you remember the exact seating arrangement of your high school biology class, but hardly anything of what you learned there?

Can you sometimes remember that a particular passage in a book you read years ago was on a left-hand page, third paragraph down?

After a particularly vivid dream, have you ever said to yourself: I will remember this in the morning. . . I will remember this in the morning. . . . And then you wake up with only a vague memory that you had some dream?

Have you ever been able to recall the number of syllables of a word, but not the word itself?

Do you know all these personal numbers by heart: Social Security, Zip code, telephone, fax, checking account, driver's license, license plate, locker combination?

Have you ever walked into a room and completely forgotten the reason you went there?

Quick! Without looking—what color tie or scarf are you wearing?

We've explored the moon. We've split the atom. But the human mind, and the memory stored within it, is still a mysterious, largely uncharted territory. Fortunately, it's a territory we're learning more about every day.

Obviously, you've selected this book because you think you have a poor memory, or you feel you can improve your memory. Good. That's an excellent start. When you have the desire to get better at something, you're well on the way to achieving your goal.

There are dozens of books on memory improvement (too many to bother remembering!).

What's different about this one?

Supermemory goes beyond the old memorization techniques and explores the latest, most successful advances made in the scientific study of memory over the last several years. By the time you finish this book, you will know about many surprising new memory improvement systems. But more important, you will be able to identify which techniques are best suited to *you*, personally.

The many methods you'll find in these pages are the result of years of work and thousands of experiments with young, middle-aged, and elderly adults, and they have proven effective for just about every type of memory situation. If you're intent on a real change in your memory ability, *Supermemory* offers you genuine, practical help.

In chapter 1, you'll learn about the development of memory improvement techniques throughout history. In chapter 2, you'll read about how your memory works. Chapter 3 tests your memory and helps you figure out which types of memory situations you especially need to work on. Chapters 4 and 5 discuss how your attitude, physical condition, and social situations influence memory. Chapters 6 and 7 cover mental strategies and external devices that enhance memory processes. Chapter 8 tells you about mental strategies that can help you handle specific memory situations. Finally, chapter 9 reveals how you can further develop your memory skills and use them with savvy in your everyday life.

Memory does *not* necessarily deteriorate slowly as we age. Your memory is probably better than you think, and you can make it better still, regardless of whether you're young, old, brilliant, or slow. All you need are the right tools and practice. The right tools are in this book.

Chapter 1

THE IMPORTANCE OF MEMORY

It's one thing if you occasionally forget where you put your house keys. It's quite another to forget the keys to your luggage when you leave home for a trip around the world. A poor memory can be worse than annoying. There are times when it can seriously disrupt your life.

"What! You Forgot Our Anniversary?"

In the business world, it's essential in most jobs to remember proper procedures, items on inventory, or where important papers are kept. Poor recall about these work matters can make you appear incompetent. Unscrupulous people will take advantage of those who don't remember things. For example, someone may borrow money from you and deliberately not repay the loan if they know you have forgotten it. When I was in the military, I learned that forgetting to lock a safe holding classified material is grounds for court-martial.

Frequent memory failures can impact your personal life, too. Heaven help the spouse who forgets an anniversary! If you forget information about the people you know, it not only hurts their feelings, but also makes you appear insensitive, self-centered, and possibly rude.

Good recall says good things about you personally.

Furthermore, memory failure can harm your well-being. If you forget to pay your bills, your credit rating is damaged. If you forget to take your medication, you may put your very life at risk. People who constantly forget simply don't feel good about themselves.

A good memory, on the other hand, will bring advantages to every part of your life. It will improve your chances for career advancement. Social relationships will run more smoothly. People will have a higher respect for you, and you'll respect yourself more—your sense of personal identity will be enriched by the large collection of experiences a good memory retains.

A Little Memory History: What Was Julius Caesar's Phone Number?

You might think that people in civilizations from the distant past didn't have many memory problems. They didn't have telephones, so they didn't have to worry about remembering anybody's phone number. They obviously didn't have to learn all the state capitals or which president came after Millard Fillmore. Memorizing history must have been a snap—there wasn't much to memorize!

But, in fact, the ancient Egyptians, Greeks, and Romans found memory problems so troubling that they created gods, such as Mnemosyne, the Greek goddess of memory, to help them remember! For thousands of years since then, various "experts" have emerged to present new ways to magnify memory.

Among the best known of these was the Greek poet, Simonides, who astounded his contemporaries in 477 B.C. with his amazing memory. The story goes that Simonides was attending a banquet when the roof of the building fell in and killed many of those unfortunate enough to have been present. In order to notify the next of kin, it was necessary to identify the banquet guests, but the bodies of the victims were damaged beyond recognition. (They didn't have dental records in those days!) Simonides came to the rescue. He was able to recall the name of every person who attended the banquet, as well as where he or she sat.

Simonides claimed he did this by imagining the people in their places at the table during the banquet. Subsequently, this method for remembering, called the *method of loci*, was regarded in ancient Greece as *the* memory tool.

If you had lived back then, you would have been told the following: When you want to memorize several pieces of information, think of a house, banquet table, or some other spatial image. Next, imagine each piece of information in a different location there. Later, when you want to recall the information, simply think of the place and you'll recall what you "left" there.

After Simonides, other memory improvement techniques were developed. The *peg system* was one of these. Instead of memorizing items by putting them into an image of a place, experts suggested putting the items on "pegs," sort of like a mental coatrack.

For example, if somebody needed to go to the store and buy milk, eggs, and bread, he could use a short rhyme like "one is a bun, two is a shoe, three is a tree." By imagining the milk sitting on a bun, a couple of eggs in a shoe, and a loaf of bread hanging from a tree, it was a snap to recite the rhyme and recall what needed to be purchased. (One had to be careful, I suppose, not to buy a bun, a shoe, and a tree.)

When you seek to improve your memory today through books and courses, chances are that you'll be taught the same old loci and peg-based methods that have been passed down through the centuries. For various reasons, the memory improvement business has not kept up with the times.

A New Approach to Memory

The ancient memory methods purport to be useful for *any* memory situation that might confront you, but research has disproved that claim. They may help you learn a list of unconnected items, but they aren't much good if you need to remember more complex material such as a poem, document, or story. In some cases, such as when you need to register someone's face in your mind, they're totally useless.

The old practice of using mental images as a memory tool works—sometimes. But modern science has more successful systems.

A growing knowledge of the different factors that affect memory has shown scientists and health-care professionals many new ways that memory can be improved. Your attitude, physical condition, mental state, conversational skills, and the use of physical memory aids can all play a role in pumping up your memory power.

Here's a quick example of how to present practical guidance for memory improvement based on the latest findings in the field.

Most people assume they can learn material best if they sit down over a concentrated period of time and study it carefully. In fact, researchers recently uncovered a better way: Look over the material you need to memorize, then let some time pass and look over it again. Now *double* the time period before you look at the material again. Keep doubling the no-study time period, then reviewing the material. These repeated exposures over time to material you want to learn will *solidify* memory more than one intensive study session will.

The basic truth behind *Supermemory* is this: There is no single magic pill or trick for all-purpose memory improvement. Instead, I will show you how to assess the state of your memory as it is right now, and then address

---

Mental manipulation is the key to total recall.

---

your specific memory problems with activities that I call manipulations, which have been designed to correct those problems.

Are you ready to improve your memory? Good. Let's get started.

Chapter 2

THE NEW MEMORY IMPROVEMENT SYSTEM

In 1959, brain surgeon William Penfield, M.D., conducted some remarkable experiments on epileptic patients. Penfield found that when he touched specific parts of the patient's brain with a weak electrical stimulation, the fully conscious patient would begin talking, shouting, and describing memories from years past—as if he or she were experiencing them all over again.

This demonstration proved that individual memories take up residence in different parts of the brain. Similarly, different portions of the brain perform different memory functions. For example, the left side of your brain handles language skills. People who have suffered brain damage in a particular area (as might result from an auto accident) may have great difficulty learning abstract concepts, but can play the piano or hit a baseball as well as they ever did.

The tissue of the brain shares something with the rest of your body—the better you treat it, the better it will treat you. Poor health, fatigue, malnourishment, and substance abuse can all lead to poor memory performance. One of the most obvious—but often neglected—ways to increase the efficiency of your memory system is to improve your physical condition.

Your physical condition impacts on your ability to remember.

The "Stereo System" of Your Mind

Sometimes it seems that there are hundreds of ways your memory can fail you, but actually there are only three. It can fail to *register* a piece of information. It can fail to *retain* information which was registered successfully. Finally, it can fail to *remember* something, even after it was successfully registered and retained. We can't always say precisely where in the brain certain memory processes occur, but we have learned quite a bit about how the processes of memory function and malfunction.

Think of your home stereo system. It is made up of several separate but connected components. You have a receiver to collect radio signals, a tuner to select parts of that signal, an amplifier to change the signals into audible sound, and speakers to broadcast the sound. Most likely you also have a turntable, tape deck, or CD player attached to your system, which provide additional sources of signals.

Many psychologists have put forth the idea that memory is made up of components much like a stereo system, with each part of the memory system having a specific job and contributing to the overall functioning.

This component system won't play the latest Prince or Pavarotti albums, but it *will* allow you to experience and remember them. There are four components to this system: the senses (your antenna, so to speak), a working memory (receiver), a long-term memory (tape deck), and a central processor (tuner). Think of your mouth as a speaker, which is not a part of the memory system.

The senses, obviously, are your sight, hearing, smell, taste, and touch. The working memory is a holding area rather than a long-term storage area. If you look up a phone number and remember it long enough to place the call, that's your working memory in action. The contents of the working memory will fade in about one minute unless a special effort is made to attend to them. The central processor controls how much attention is given to the contents of the working memory. Perceptions and memories that are given special attention and last far beyond that one minute reside in the long-term memory. This is where, like your collection of treasured oldies, memories can be pulled out and replayed again and again.

Anything given less than one minute of thought will fade from your memory.

So, basically, a memory *trace*, or remnant of experience, is registered according to a certain sequence. Information in the world around us is picked up by the senses and transferred to working memory. The information may or may not make it to the long-term memory, depending on how the central processor treats it. This brings us conveniently to the most important process of that stereo system in your head.

Attention and Retention

It should not come as a huge shock to hear that the most important process of the memory system is *attention.* That mean third-grade teacher you hated so much had it right: "If you don't pay attention, you won't learn." The likelihood that information in your working memory will be absorbed into long-term memory depends on how intensely you pay attention. When you pay better attention to a working memory, the information will be clearer, more details will be registered into long-term memory, and the likelihood of remembering them later will increase. So, if you can find a way to raise your level of attention, you can enhance the quality of your memory performance.

But the level of attention is not the only aspect of attention that can go up and down. Have you ever gone to a movie because you wanted to see a particular actor or actress? You were probably watching that one star so intently that you didn't notice the supporting actors, the sets, or the background music very much. Even though your *level* of attention was high, your memories of the movie in general are probably quite low.

In all aspects of our everyday life, we pay more attention to some details than to others. Naturally, those details that get the most attention are more likely to be remembered than the details we ignore. We are *distributing* our attention quite willfully over the contents of our working memory.

So it is the general *level* of your attention plus the way your attention is *distributed* that combine to determine how much of a particular piece of information you will remember.

Mind manipulation requires two skills: level of attention and distribution of attention.

What do you remember of the movie *Gone With The Wind*? The answer is a function of how interested you were in seeing the film to begin with (your level of attention) and which details—costumes, actors, settings, and so forth—you may have been particularly interested in while you were watching it (your distribution of attention).

This distinction between the level of attention and the distribution of attention is important to memory improvement. Here's why: Some of the techniques you're going to learn in this book will increase your level of attention, but will have no effect on your distribution of attention. With others, it will be the reverse. To have a good memory, it is necessary to be able to set a high level of attention *and* to control the way your attention is distributed. To maximize your memory performance, it's necessary to work on both kinds of manipulations of attention.

Influence and Memory

Remembering someone's birthday may seem the same as remembering an appointment, but in fact they're subtly different tasks for your memory system. The appointment involves more information (date *and* time), while the birthday carries with it more personal significance.

Different kinds of memory situations challenge us in various ways, and how well we remember something depends critically on how well our memory techniques, which we call manipulations, meet the needs of that particular situation. Later, we'll see that these subtle differences make it worthwhile to register birthdays and appointments in memory using different mental procedures.

Three things influence your attention when you try to remember something: external forces, the type of information you're trying to learn, and intentionality.

Matter over Mind

External forces fall under four categories:

1. *Your physical and mental condition.* If you're in a cheerful, positive state of mind, it's easier to learn someone's name than if you're feeling tired, negative, or depressed.
2. *The social context.* The presence of others often inspires us to try harder in memory situations than when we are alone. Moreover, when we're with other people, there are memory situations that simply don't come up when we're alone. For example, you try to remember not to mention an ex-wife or husband when socializing with a recently divorced friend.

Your memory has to work harder when you're in the presence of others.

3. *The physical environment.* You may find that you study better outdoors or while listening to a certain type of music. Certain objects, signs, and visual patterns can activate memories far better than others. The same is true for certain sounds and odors. Some commercial products are sold explicitly as memory aids. Alarm clocks, for instance, are generally more accurate than biological clocks, and appliances that automatically switch themselves off when left unattended eliminate the necessity even to remember certain things.
4. *Mental limitations.* The amount of information and the way it is presented influence how effectively your memory processes are able to handle it. It's more difficult to memorize a 50-line poem than a haiku. It's tougher to memorize stock market symbols if they flash by on a screen than if they are printed on a sheet of paper. It's harder to learn a list of words if they are printed in a foreign language than if they are printed in your own language.

Just How Important Is It?

The second characteristic that affects attention is the type of material you're trying to learn or remember. A game like Trivial Pursuit, for example, requires memory for basic *knowledge*. Reminiscing with your friends about the good old days draws on your memory for *events*. Remembering an appointment or someone's birthday requires that you remember an *intention*. And anything from throwing a football to doing the fox-trot depends on your memory for *actions*.

Try to Remember...

You've probably had the experience of noticing that you know all the words to a certain song, despite the fact that you never made any effort to learn them. When you learn something without conscious awareness in this manner, it is called performing a memory task *incidentally*. On the other hand, when you deliberately direct your attention to what you want to remember, you are performing a memory task *intentionally*.

Our memories are filled with a lot of things we never even meant to remember.

The distinction between intentional and incidental learning does have practical importance. On the average, when you learn something intentionally, the memory trace will be more detailed and useful. You are more likely to remember something if you learned it intentionally than if you learned it incidentally.

The New Theory of Memory Improvement

Let's say you want to improve your skill at tennis. You wouldn't work just on your backhand. If you were truly serious about improving your game, you'd tackle it from all angles. You'd get in shape. You'd learn about rackets, court surfaces, and equipment. You'd learn tennis strategy. You'd learn about your opponents and which tactics work best against specific players. You'd identify which of your shots need the most work, learn how to make them, and practice regularly.

Improving your memory calls for a similar approach. A single method isn't going to help you achieve mastery.

The best formula involves a variety of factors: conditioning, emotions, social context, and street smarts, as well as mental techniques.

Some memory improvement methods concentrate exclusively on mental techniques. This is like deciding to improve your tennis game, but working only on your backhand. The approach to memory improvement I present here is more comprehensive than traditional methods.

In the next chapter, we'll test your memory to find out which situations are giving you the most trouble. After that, you'll see what you can do to improve them.

Summary

Memory improvement depends on the components of your memory system and how well they work together.

You can help your memory system work better by raising your level of attention for the things you want to remember and by distributing your attention through memory techniques called manipulations.

This book will help you develop a repertoire of manipulations and learn which ones to use for specific memory situations.

Chapter 3

HOW GOOD IS YOUR MEMORY?

"I have a good memory."

"I have a bad memory."

"I have a *terrible* memory."

Most people think they know how well their memory works, but research has proven that they're very often wrong. Studies show that people who say they don't remember names, for example, are often *good* at remembering names.

One reason we're so poor at evaluating our memory is because society has trained us to believe that memory ability, like a muscle, is either strong or weak. In fact, nobody's memory is uniformly good or bad across all situations. Most people are good at some memory tasks and bad at others. If someone is known to have a "good memory," it usually means he or she has a knack for a particular memory *task*, such as remembering dates. Similarly, people are often unfairly saddled with the reputation of a "bad memory" simply because they tend to forget something obvious—birthdays, for instance.

The other reason we don't have an accurate impression of our memory abilities is because we don't keep systematic records of how often we succeed or fail at memory tasks. Before you can improve your memory, you have to assess exactly which memory tasks give you trouble. Once you know that, you can attempt to improve on those abilities. And when you find which memory tasks you perform well, you will have new confidence about them and avoid wasting effort to improve them. A realistic evaluation of your memory ability puts you in the right position to work at making it better.

Your memory is better than you think. The challenge is in finding your memory weaknesses.

Standard Ways to Measure Your Memory

The *best* way to have your memory evaluated is to be tested by a professional—usually a psychologist, but sometimes a neurologist or a psychiatrist. Most likely, he or she will give you the Wechsler Memory Scale test which asks you to recall current events, a list of digits, words, word pairs, a short story, and a geometric pattern. Other respected memory tests incorporate tasks more like those encountered in everyday life, such as remembering appointments or a route to get somewhere.

Unfortunately, professional memory testing is expensive, time-consuming, and intimidating for some people. And though you obviously have an interest in improving your memory, are you willing to pay a professional to help you do it?

(If you wish to take a formal memory-performance examination by a professional, call the psychology department or educational psychology department of the nearest large university and ask to speak to the psychologist who specializes in memory. If the person you reach does not do memory assessment, he or she will probably refer you to someone who can. Some neurologists or psychiatrists also have the appropriate background, but you're more likely to get a thorough—and less expensive—examination from a psychologist.)

When asked which president said "The buck stops here," few people give the correct answer: Truman.

Many books contain memory improvement tests that can be self-administered or given to you by a friend. The tests in these books are much like those used by professionals. Unfortunately, the results you get are not as reliable. For memory test results to be accurate, the test has to be administered in a very precise manner. The person giving the test must allow a certain number of seconds to present each item, a certain number of seconds between items, and a certain number of seconds for recall.

Additionally, all subjects must be examined under the same environmental conditions. A professional knows how to give a test in a uniform way to everyone and how to take into account factors that may have a negative effect on your performance, such as *test anxiety*, nervousness that inhibits memory performance during a test, or *guessing biases*, the tendency to choose the most familiar possibility when you don't know the correct answer. If you ask people, for example, "Which president said 'The buck stops here'?" they're likely to reply Nixon, Kennedy, or Johnson. They rarely get the correct answer: Truman.

The All-New Memory Test

There is now a test that promises to be more sophisticated, extensive, and substantially superior to previous self-administered memory tests. I've created this questionnaire so you can judge your performance in the four categories of memory tasks we encounter in everyday life: *knowledge, events, intentions, and actions.*

Knowledge

Throughout the course of your life, you are exposed to a tremendous amount of information—in school, of course, but also in your job, your hobbies, and through the media. Depending on your personal interests, you naturally learn more about some subjects than you do about others. You might avoid some subjects entirely or never have the opportunity to learn about them.

Score your personal college of knowledge. You may not realize the wealth of your memory bank.

How Much Do You Think You Know and Remember?

Below is a list of many topics—various aspects of knowledge. For each one, first indicate whether you ever studied or took an interest in the topic in your lifetime. If you think you *did* study this topic, circle "Yes." If not, circle "No."

To the right of each "Yes" answer, estimate the degree of confidence you have in your ability to answer a question about that topic right now.

For example, if you *think* that you would almost *always* remember the answer to a question on the topic, write the number 1 in the space provided. This indicates that you feel your memory is excellent for the topic. If you think that you would almost *always* forget, write 7. If you think you would remember the answer about half the time, write 4. Writing a 2 or 3 indicates you would remember answers on this topic more than half the time, but not all. A 5 or 6 indicates you would remember answers to less than half of the questions on this topic. Remember, answer "Yes" or "No" to *all* the topics, and place a number next to each "Yes" answer.

1-Always   **5-Now and then**
2-Very often   **6-Once in a while**
3-Fairly often   **7-Never**
4-About half the time

Agriculture	Yes	No	Rating: _____
Anthropology	Yes	No	Rating: _____
Art	Yes	No	Rating: _____
Biology	Yes	No	Rating: _____
Chemistry	Yes	No	Rating: _____
Cooking	Yes	No	Rating: _____
Current events	Yes	No	Rating: _____

Drama	Yes	No	Rating: _____
Economics	Yes	No	Rating: _____
English	Yes	No	Rating: _____
Etiquette	Yes	No	Rating: _____
Foreign languages	Yes	No	Rating: _____
Geography	Yes	No	Rating: _____
Geology	Yes	No	Rating: _____
History	Yes	No	Rating: _____
Hobbies	Yes	No	Rating: _____
Home repairs	Yes	No	Rating: _____
Hygiene	Yes	No	Rating: _____
Jokes	Yes	No	Rating: _____
Law	Yes	No	Rating: _____
Literature	Yes	No	Rating: _____
Mathematics	Yes	No	Rating: _____
Music	Yes	No	Rating: _____
Past news	Yes	No	Rating: _____
Philosophy	Yes	No	Rating: _____
Physics	Yes	No	Rating: _____
Politics	Yes	No	Rating: _____
Reading books	Yes	No	Rating: _____
Religion	Yes	No	Rating: _____
Sculpture	Yes	No	Rating: _____
Social studies	Yes	No	Rating: _____
Sociology	Yes	No	Rating: _____
Spelling	Yes	No	Rating: _____
Sports	Yes	No	Rating: _____
Theater	Yes	No	Rating: _____
Trivia	Yes	No	Rating: _____

Also, how well do you know:

Commonly used phone numbers	Yes	No	Rating: _____
Information learned on a job	Yes	No	Rating: _____

How to get around places   Yes No Rating: _____
you once lived
Names of famous people   Yes No Rating: _____
Names of people known   Yes No Rating: _____
for a long time

Events

There are about three billion individuals on this planet, but not a single one of them has a life exactly like yours. Our experiences are essential to how we perceive ourselves. What we have or have not done determines who we are. How well we remember is important to all of us.

Your life is filled with millions of experiences you easily forget. A trained mind will reward you with many additional memories.

How Is Your Memory for Everyday Details?

Inevitably, we forget many of our life experiences, either partially or entirely. This questionnaire asks you to estimate how often you remember details in your everyday life. Put a number from 1 to 7 to indicate how often you remember the following experiences.

1-Always   **5-Now and then**
2-Very often   **6-Once in a while**
3-Fairly often   **7-Never**
4-About half the time

1. Think of the times you need to remember a phone number or an address you read just moments before. How

often do you remember it without having to check the source again? _____

2. How often are you able to recall the names of people you know? _____

3. How often are you able to recall the names of people you met minutes earlier? _____

4. When you put something down and go to look for it a little while later, how often do you remember where you put it? _____

5. When friends and relatives discuss events from your childhood, how often do you remember the incidents they are talking about? _____

6. When you're in a restaurant and want to speak to your server, how often are you able to remember what he or she looks like? _____

7. How often do you remember what someone has just said to you? _____

8. Think of times when someone gave you directions to a destination. How often do you remember them on your way there? _____

9. When someone says he has told you something at an earlier time, how often can you remember what he said and when he said it? _____

10. After watching a movie or television show, how often are you able to remember the details? _____

Intentions

Famous last words: "Don't forget to pick up a carton of milk on your way home from work." There are many times when you need to remember to do something for yourself or for others. Sometimes, of course, you don't remember to do it. When you forget your obligations, you risk embarrassment and the ill will of others involved.

It's easy to forget what you don't want to remember. But it can have negative repercussions.

How Good Are You at Remembering to Follow Through on Intentions?

This questionnaire asks you to estimate how often you remember the things you intend to do.

1-Always	**5-Now and then**
2-Very often	**6-Once in a while**
3-Fairly often	**7-Never**
4-About half the time	

1. How often do you remember things that you were supposed to do? _____

2. When you have an errand or several things to do but do not make a written reminder, how often do you remember to do all the items on your mental list? _____

3. Think of times when you go to a room to get something. How often do you get to the room knowing why you are there? _____

4. When you go out, how often do you remember what you needed to bring along without having to return for an item? _____

5. How often do you remember appointments? _____

6. When someone asks you to tell something to a mutual acquaintance, how often do you remember to do so? _____

7. When you are supposed to take an item with you (to work, a club, or school), how often do you remember to do so? _____

8. How often do you remember routine chores (such as taking out the garbage, picking up the mail, or locking up the house)? _____

9. How often do you remember to take along personal possessions that you usually carry with you (wallet, purse, glasses, keys, pens, medicine, and such)? _____

10. How often do you remember to follow through on commonplace actions, such as turning off a faucet, taking a pot off a burner, or fastening parts of your clothing? _____

Actions

It's easier to fix a toaster if you can remember how you fixed one in the past. Many tasks in daily life require us to recall *actions*. An accurate memory for actions can serve you well in a variety of situations, ranging from house repairs to athletics.

A good memory for recalling how to do things can make life a whole lot easier.

How Good Are You at Remembering Necessary Steps in Common Tasks?

This questionnaire asks you to estimate how often you remember how to perform actions in your everyday life.

1-Always   **5-Now and then**
2-Very often   **6-Once in a while**
3-Fairly often   **7-Never**
4-About half the time

1. Think of times you want to perform a certain movement you used to do a long time ago (like a dance step or a particular shot in a sport). How often do you get the movement just right? _____

2. Sometimes you have people show you how to do things. Other times, you read a do-it-yourself book. How often are you able to remember and reproduce an action you're learning? _____

3. How often are you able to perform the correct action without confusing it with a similar action you know from before (for example, shifting gears on a new car the way you shifted them on a previous car, or swinging a racket in tennis as you might in squash)? _____

4. How often do you remember to include all of the steps in an action (as in reassembling something you've taken apart)? _____

5. When performing an action that involves several steps, how often do you remember which step comes next? _____

6. How often do you remember how to perform everyday actions (such as which way to turn the key in a lock, or which button to use on an appliance)? _____

7. How often are you able to remember every step for an action that involves several steps (such as combining ingredients when cooking)? _____

8. Think of times when someone gave you directions for doing some action (such as how to fix something, or how to assemble a product that comes unassembled). How often do you remember the latter part of the directions even if you have difficulty carrying out the initial steps? _____

9. When you're doing something that requires several items (such as tools for a repair job, or ingredients when cooking), how often do you pick up the correct thing for the next step? _____

10. Some actions require various tools, parts, or ingredients. How often do you remember every tool you need at the start without having to interrupt your activity and get something needed to complete the project? _____

Knowing the Score

For the questions you've just answered, most people mark 2's or 3's, indicating that they remember things "Very often" to "Fairly often." The difficult part about evaluating tests like this is that the responses often reflect how kind a person is to himself or herself just as much as they reflect that person's level of ability. Some people judge their average performance to be near perfection, while others tend to be quite hard on themselves.

The aim here is to discover which memory tasks give you the *most* problems. In each section, put a check mark next to the two questions that deal with areas in which you rated your memory performance the poorest and in which you wish to improve. If you're *not* interested in improving at a particular task, don't pick that question. (Many people are willing to accept a poor performance in certain tasks, and they have no desire to get better in them. For example, some people don't care to memorize the name of a person on the first meeting. They prefer to wait until they know a person better before making an effort to register the name in memory.)

Dear Diary . . .

Questionnaires provide a good way to take stock of our memory abilities. But very often we forget or remember things without our really noticing it, so it's important to realize that your answers are not 100 percent accurate.

To supplement the questionnaire you just answered, I suggest keeping a *memory diary* for a direct account of how your memory actually performs. A memory diary generally yields more accurate information about your ability to remember than a questionnaire does, because diary entries are made shortly after a memory task whereas a questionnaire is usually filled out much later. Also, a diary can either corroborate or challenge the answers on a questionnaire. By keeping a diary, you may very well discover that some aspects of your memory are better or worse than you suspected.

Keeping a memory diary for one month will reveal the areas in which your ability to recall is weak or strong.

Keeping a regular diary can be a tedious chore, but a memory diary is relatively simple. I'd like you to make 30 photocopies of the Memory Daily Record on the opposite page and carry one copy with you every day for the next month. Instead of writing a memory diary from scratch, simply fill in the blanks on these sheets of paper.

I chose the memory tasks listed in the diary because they are important to most people and because they're fairly easy to observe. If you like, add other memory tasks to the sheet.

During the next month, note on your daily page *every time your memory fails you.* If you miss an appointment, record it in your memory diary. If you forget someone's name, record that as well. Put a check mark next to the category of that memory failure and jot down a few words to describe it. That way, you can think about the event and possibly avoid a similar memory failure in the future.

A memory failure might occur while you're with

other people. If you feel awkward about pulling out your diary, slip into a rest room or enter a note in the diary as soon as you're alone. But don't rely on remembering to fill in the diary sometime later. The longer you delay, the greater the chance that you'll forget, making your diary less accurate than it could be.

Memory Daily Record

Memory Task	**Description of memory failure (day and date)**
Knowledge	
Background Data. You forgot some information you learned while in school, at work, or in some less formal situation.	_____ _____ _____ _____ _____
Events	
Recent Data. You needed to remember a phone number or address you read out of a book moments before, but you forgot some or all of it and had to check again.	_____ _____ _____ _____ _____ _____
Names You Know. You couldn't recall the name of a person you know.	_____ _____ _____
Recent Events. You forgot details of a movie, show, or event while discussing it with people who also observed the event.	_____ _____ _____ _____

Intentions

Forgot What to Do.
You knew you were sup-
posed to do something,
but forgot what it was.
    _____

Forgot Something.
When going out, you dis-
covered that you had to
return for something you
intended to take but left
behind.
    _____

Actions

Weakened Skill. You
wanted to do a certain
movement that you hav-
en't done in a long time,
but you couldn't get it just
right.
    _____

Missed Step. You left
out a step in an action or
series of actions.
    _____

Adding It Up

When the month is over, use a separate sheet to total
up the number of times you failed at each type of memory
task. These totals will help indicate which tasks are easiest
or hardest for you.

But before you draw any firm conclusions, it's important to consider how many times you confronted each
memory task. An educated guess will do. Research indi-

cates that estimates made after a diary is written are sufficiently accurate. If you were introduced to 500 people last month and forgot the names of 50 of them, it wouldn't be fair to say you have a poor memory for names. On the other hand, if you met 50 people last month and forgot *all* of their names, that's a pretty dismal performance. In both cases, you forgot 50 names, so you can see that the number of memory failures alone is not a fair measure of your ability.

That's why it's necessary to convert these raw numbers of memory failures into a rating that reflects how often you confronted each task. Use the same 7-point scale you used previously to grade your questionnaire. A number 1 indicates that you *always* remembered during the diary period (relative to the number of opportunities for failure you encountered). Number 7 indicates that you *never* remembered. So if you had 10 memory failures out of an estimated 20 chances at the task, your success rate would be "About half the time" (a rating of 4). If you had only 1 memory failure in 20 chances, the success rate would be "Always" (1) or "Very often" (2).

Do this for every category on your memory diary. Next, record your ratings of your diary experiences on the sheet where you have written your diary totals.

These ratings will be used later for a comprehensive analysis of your memory performance.

Interpreting Results

By now, you realize that you can't just say, "I want a better memory," and work from there. It's not as simple as that because different techniques of memory improvement work better on different memory tasks.

You need a realistic view of your memory trouble spots in order to take corrective action.

The trick is to match up your most vexing memory problems with techniques that are most likely to help you overcome them. Comparing your scores from the questionnaire and the diary should give you a good idea of which specific memory situations are your strongest and which ones need improvement.

Before you rush to the next chapter, consider which of the categories—knowledge, events, intentions, actions— are most important to your memory goals and which matter least to you. Next, look at your questionnaire and diary answers to see how you actually performed in each of those categories. If you marked low numbers (1 through 4) in the Knowledge section for both the diary and the questionnaire, it indicates your memory for knowledge is already quite good and probably doesn't need much work. If you have high numbers (5 through 7), it's obvious that this kind of material gives you trouble.

Chances are, your questionnaire and diary ratings will agree fairly well. But if your questionnaire and diary ratings differ, give greater weight to the diary estimates, since we know that diaries are generally more accurate than questionnaires. For example, if you recorded that you have difficulty remembering names on the questionnaire but the diary shows little difficulty in remembering names, it's safe to conclude that you are probably better with names than you thought.

If there is a big difference between the results of your questionnaire and the entries in your diary, it's likely that your assessment of your memory abilities was not on the mark before you started keeping the diary.

Nevertheless, you may *still* feel that your questionnaire responses are more accurate than your diary. If you do, continue to keep the diary until you're convinced about the true nature of your memory abilities.

Different memory problems require different techniques to overcome them.

There's one other thing I'd like you to do. Remember when you filled in the questionnaire and I asked you to put a check mark next to two questions from each section in which you rated your memory performance the poorest? When you complete your diary, go back to those check marks and compare them. Check to see how your scores match up. Do you *still* feel those are the areas that give you the most problems? If so, write them down in Memory Trouble Spots on page 34. If not, you should now be in a position to determine the memory situations/categories that you feel you need to work on the most. Write *them* down.

After answering all the questions and faithfully keeping your diary, you'll know your most troublesome memory tasks—the problems you'll need to pay special attention to as you read the remainder of this book.

Memory Trouble Spots

1. _____

_____

2. _____

_____

3. _____

_____

4. _____

_____

Summary

Most of us are only partially aware of our memory abilities. We often avoid memory tasks at which we could succeed and take on others we should skip. Our tendency to tackle or avoid a memory task depends on how we view our memory abilities.

To improve these memory abilities, you need a realistic knowledge of your strengths and weaknesses.

You can achieve this knowledge by carefully completing a comprehensive questionnaire and by keeping a memory diary. These will give you a better idea of how your memory performs on a day-to-day basis and help you set goals for memory improvement.

Chapter 4

GETTING YOUR MEMORY IN PEAK CONDITION

It's four in the morning. You're at your high school class's ten-year reunion. You've had a few drinks and you haven't slept in nearly 24 hours. An old friend from your junior year biology class strolls over and greets you enthusiastically. Do you think you're going to remember this person's name?

Don't bet on it.

Research shows that overall memory performance can range from good to poor depending on a person's physical and/or mental condition. In fact, *your health is the single most important factor in how you perform on incidental memory tasks*—that is, those memories you store when you're not intentionally trying to remember something. It is also a major factor in your performance of intentional memory tasks.

The high school reunion scenario is an unusual example, of course, but even in everyday tasks your mental and physical condition can have a major impact on your memory system. A business deal settled over a two-martini lunch may seem hazy a day later. Late nights studying often result in fatigue, which interferes with remembering whatever you learned.

Running yourself ragged one day can give you a foggy brain the day after. Your chances of stocking your long-term memory diminish greatly.

Poor Health, Poor Memory

When your mental and physical conditions are poor, your *entire* memory system functions under par. Attention, a key to memory performance, is diminished. Long-term memory suffers. The central processor doesn't fully attend to the contents of working memory, so ideas and images are not likely to be registered strongly. Memory traces become fainter. It's harder to get them into or out of long-term memory. To restore your memory system to full function, it's necessary to improve the condition of body and mind. For some people, this may mean major lifestyle changes.

If you picked up this book thinking it would reveal fast and easy solutions to your memory problems, you should know that there are no quick fixes. But if you *really* want to improve your memory performance, the suggestions in this chapter will pay off.

As with your body, you can't get your memory in shape without a little mental grunting and sweating.

Exercise Your Mind

People who frequently get sick have significantly more memory problems than people who stay in good health, according to a survey of 1,000 people done by the National Center of Health Statistics.

Healthy people have fewer memory problems than people who frequently get sick. People who exercise are healthier than people who don't.

Exercise helps you maintain your strength and cardiovascular condition, keeping you physically ready for memory tasks. It helps relieve you of the "blues," lessens stress, improves digestion, improves sleep—all of which help memory.

It may seem silly to exercise *just* to improve your memory. Most people exercise for other reasons—this gives you one more.

I realize that the mere thought of exercise makes some people want to go lie down and rest. I'm not suggesting you start pumping iron or running ten miles for the sake of your memory. A 20-minute walk each day is probably sufficient for a person who doesn't exercise regularly otherwise. The thing is to get out, move your body around, get your blood circulating, and shake up those old and new memories.

Your Memory Has a Clock

Have you ever heard somebody say he's a "night person" or a "morning person"? That's not just imagination talking. Our strength for memory tasks is cyclical. There are certain times of the day and certain days of the week when memory functions best.

I call these *peak times*. Over the years I've discovered that I'm able to do my best work between 10:30 A.M. and 1:00 P.M. It's not that I'm useless the rest of the day, but in the morning I feel mentally sharpest and can accomplish more. Everyone has a personal peak time, and most people find that time comes somewhere between 11:00 A.M. and 4:00 P.M.

There are a few reasons why we have this peak. As the day goes on, we gradually get more involved with our daily activities. After lunch time, general fatigue starts to set in, and we lose our edge later in the day. Our daily biological cycles—body temperature, respiration, and pulse rate—also vary our powers of attentiveness.

Your sleep schedule affects your daily peaks for memory tasks, too. If you go to bed early and get up early, you probably learn more readily at the beginning of the day. If you go to bed late and get up late, it's the opposite. When I was teaching full time, my peak hours came in the early afternoon. When I did research at the National Institute of Mental Health, I got up at 6:00 A.M. and my peak hours moved up to an earlier time. If you work a night shift or on weekends, your peak times are probably different from those of people who work nine to five, Monday through Friday.

Although the typical peak time for memory performance occurs around the middle of the day, it may very well be different for you. You can judge what times are peak for you simply by paying attention to when you feel most alert and can think most clearly.

Take advantage of your peak time. You can make the best use of your reserves of strength by performing memory tasks when these reserves are at their highest. If you do creative or mental work, try to do it during your peak time. If you have control over meetings, schedule them to your advantage. Set aside your drudge work—opening mail, tidying up your office, and so on—and do it during off-peak times.

There are certain times of the day and certain days of the week when your memory functions at its best. Save creative and mental work for your peak hours.

Additionally, try to schedule important learning tasks toward the end of the week. Strangely enough, research shows that, for most people, memory ability tends to be at its best on Friday and Saturday. This is probably because the anticipation of the weekend perks up a person's mood.

Disruptions to your daily cycle will hamper your learning and memory ability. For example, if you have an infant who wakes up every few hours during the night and interrupts your sleep, it works against your memory's efficiency the next day. Jet lag has been known to have a similar effect. If your cycle is disrupted by traveling across time zones, you may find it hard to remember directions on how to get to your hotel, or what room number the hotel desk clerk just gave you.

Disruptions in your daily life will affect your ability to learn and remember.

When there's a shift in your daily or weekly cycle, try to cut down on the number of memory tasks you have. There's not much you can do about a crying baby other than wait for it to grow, but when you travel you can allow for extra time to recuperate before taking on major tasks that rely on intellect and memory.

Sleep on It

A number of years ago, a popular theory held that people could learn while they were asleep. Not only that, proponents of this theory insisted that people remembered material *better* if they learned it while sleeping than if they learned it while awake. Clever entrepreneurs probably made millions from people who bought records and tapes and drifted off to dreamland in hopes of waking up with encyclopedias, dictionaries, and even foreign languages firmly memorized.

A great deal of research on this topic shows clearly: People do not learn while asleep. If you play a tape during the night and learn some of the material, you are actually remembering what you heard during a wake period. When you are truly asleep, you learn *nothing*.

Some evidence shows that if you go to sleep immediately *after* you learn something, however, you'll remember more of it than if you stay up and do something, like play cards or go out to eat. So if you can arrange it, study until lights-out, then dive into bed and go to sleep.

If you study immediately before going to sleep, your ability to remember what you learned will be greater the next day.

In general, a good night's sleep will make you strong and alert for memory tasks. So get sufficient sleep before an exam or an interview if you want to be on top of your game. We can all recall occasions when we had to "pull an all-nighter" and struggled the next day to come up with words and answers that we would otherwise have remembered easily.

To ensure a good night's sleep, avoid eating and drinking late at night, avoid thinking about your troubles prior to bedtime, and go to bed at approximately the same time every night.

One more thing—avoid sleeping pills. The sleep they induce seldom refreshes as natural sleep does. Also, their carryover effect makes you less able to register new memories the next day and less susceptible to stimulation that might help you remember things you already know.

Foods for Thought

Back in the fifteenth century, experts advised people who wanted to improve their memory to eat roasted fowls and young hares, as well as apples, nuts, and red wine. To the medieval mind, hearty fare was the source of strength, energy, and increased mental powers. And these were items of choice. Our ancestors may have missed the mark with the foods they recommended, but there is no doubt they were right in thinking that nutrition played an important part in memory performance.

Today we know that food influences brain chemistry which, in turn, affects memory. Proper amounts of protein, carbohydrates, lecithin, and vitamin B_1, in particular, are considered essential to the chemical processes that occur in the brain when we register, retain, and remember. What we don't know is which foods, if any, are more "memory nutritious" than others. Therefore, it makes sense to eat a variety of fresh foods (dairy products, bread and cereals, vegetables and fruits, seafood, poultry and/or meat) as some insurance for proper memory functioning.

If your diet is lacking in certain types of foods, you might want to investigate with your doctor the value of using nutritional supplements. The so-called memory nutrients include choline, B-complex vitamins (especially B_1, B_6, and B_{12}), iodine, manganese, folic acid, and L-tyrosine. While nutrients are known to affect memory, I am not convinced that using any one vitamin or mineral has an especially beneficial effect on your ability to remember.

B vitamins are prominent among the memory nutrients.

But recent findings concerning one food substance, glucose, may force me to revise my opinion. Researchers at the University of Virginia found that drinking lemonade sweetened with glucose right after studying facilitated later recall. This result has been confirmed in other experiments by other scientists. Apparently glucose helps with the chemical processes that register long-term memories in the brain. The same can probably be said of any sugar drink, but that possibility is yet to be tested.

University of Virginia researchers found that drinking sweetened lemonade after studying improved memory performance.

My personal feeling is that most people eat a diet that provides enough of the nutrients needed for normal memory performance. If for some reason you suspect that a nutritional disorder is affecting your memory, I think you should consult a physician about the best way to correct the problem.

One further fact about food and memory: Eating large amounts of food directly before attacking a task impairs performance. Heavy eating tends to make you logy and inattentive during registration and remembering. So whatever you decide to eat, nutritious or not, be careful not to stuff yourself before taking a test, making a speech, or doing anything else that requires your memory to be at its best.

Common Sense Problems

Maybe you don't have a memory problem at all. Maybe you have a *sensory* problem. Frequently, poor eyesight or hearing prevents a person from doing well on memory tasks. Sensory difficulties slow down the initial registration of information and make it harder to notice cues that can aid remembering. In other words, if you don't hear or see something clearly, how can you hope to remember it clearly?

Sensory problems, such as poor vision, can slow down your ability to learn and remember because your mind misses many of the cues that help to register information.

If you think one of your senses may have suffered a partial loss, by all means get yourself examined by a physician. You may discover that all you really need is a loudness booster for your telephone or a magnifying glass for reading fine print. If it turns out that you need eyeglasses or a hearing aid, the improved performance they bring you will more than make up for any inconvenience in wearing them.

People tend to think that memory failures occur *only* because of memory problems. They may *assume* you have a bad memory when what you really have is bad eyesight. You probably know of children who had problems in school until it was discovered that their impaired vision prevented them from reading the blackboard.

Many children and adults conceal medical problems, so it's not surprising when others attribute memory lapses to poor memory rather than to a sensory problem. Unfortunately, when a person explains honestly that he can't remember something because he wasn't able to see or hear it in the first place, it may be regarded as a weak excuse.

Illness: A Mental Setback

Have you ever come down with a bad cold on the day you had to give a speech from memory? Chances are, you had difficulty remembering much of what you wanted to say.

We all get sick from time to time. When we do, mental tasks, including memory tasks, become more difficult. Illnesses cause discomfort, which diminishes how well we attend to things. When our ability to pay attention is lessened, we don't register information or remember it as well. Even a minor illness can impair your memory performance.

If you have a big interview or exam coming up and you're sick, try to get it postponed. There's no way you'll be at your best. If a postponement is impossible, at least make sure that you're as well rested as possible.

Being sick guarantees impaired memory performance. If you have a test or important meeting scheduled, get it postponed.

If you're taking medication for your ailment, check to see if it has side effects that influence memory. Medicines are rarely identified as interfering with memory per se. But if a drug diminishes your capacity to pay attention, it's usually pointed out on the label. In such situations, ask your pharmacist or physician if you could take another medication.

Altered States of Mind

"I drink to forget" is an old movie cliché, but it is the absolute truth in several ways. Alcohol has such an adverse effect on the memory system that it is sometimes called amnesia food.

Simply put, alcohol slowly but surely destroys brain tissue. In the brain stem, it impairs the process of absorbing information. The information never makes it into long-term memory. This tissue loss stops when alcohol intake stops, but no medicine now available can restore the lost tissue.

Alcohol randomly destroys brain cells and interferes with brain chemistry. The result: A lot of wanted information never makes it to your long-term memory.

Naturally, when brain cells are randomly destroyed by alcohol, some of the memories that disappear *are* unhappy ones. Sadly, excessive drinking not only impairs brain chemistry but also provides an excuse to "forget" unpleasant memories and antisocial acts performed during the binge.

An occasional drink is relatively harmless, but prolonged use of alcohol causes permanent damage to a person's memory system. Frequent and extensive memory loss from drink foretells the onset of a severe drinking problem.

While marijuana has not been shown to destroy brain cells, its effect right before a memory task is quite similar to that of alcohol. In an experiment conducted by John Darley, Ph. D., at Stanford University in 1973, subjects were given marijuana in pill form and asked to memorize a series of digits. The performance of the subjects under the influence of marijuana was significantly poorer than that of subjects who did not receive any drug. The researchers concluded that marijuana impairs memory.

Cocaine, crack, and other substances stronger than marijuana have an even more severe effect on intellectual functioning.

Have you ever heard someone say that he can remember something he learned under the influence of alcohol or drugs more easily if he has a few drinks or a few puffs on a joint before he tries? This is called the *state-dependent* effect on memory. According to this theory, you perform better if you learn *and* recall information while in the same state, and poorer when you try to recall a memory while in a state *different* from the one in which it was registered.

Research on alcohol and marijuana suggests a very small effect of state dependency and provides inconsistent support for it.

All in all, you'll remember information better if you don't indulge. People often say that drink or drugs helps them relax and that they can learn better when relaxed. But regardless of any moral considerations or the legality of various substances, the message of research is clear— alcohol and marijuana impair memory performance.

Coffee and Cigarette Alert

Who hasn't used a cup of coffee to perk up in the morning or stay alert while studying? The good news is that if you feel sleepy and must learn information by a certain deadline, a mild stimulant may help you stay awake and pay attention at least somewhat.

The bad news is that stimulants are just as likely to have a *negative* effect on memory as a positive one. If you're wide awake and well rested, stimulation from caffeine or nicotine will do little to enhance your memory performance. Even if they *did* work at some level, no one knows what that ideal dose would be. When you have too much of a stimulant you become jittery, find it difficult to sleep, and your memory performance suffers. For a habitual or addicted user, having to go *without* a stimulant will have the same effect.

Several years ago, I did some experiments at Hamilton College in Clinton, New York, in which students attempted to learn a list of words briefly presented to them. Half the students drank two or more cups of regular coffee or tea before being tested, and the rest drank decaffeinated coffee or tea. In three separate studies, there was essentially no difference in the performance of the two groups of students.

Some recent research suggests that caffeine may hinder memory only in *females*, but that finding has not been verified in other studies. No experiments have examined the effect of nonprescription caffeine-based stimulants, such as No-Doz and Vivarin, on memory.

Recent research indicates very clearly that smoking can impair memory performance, about as much as a couple of drinks can. Nonsmokers are quicker than smokers at remembering a list of digits. They also score higher on the standard Wechsler Memory Scale.

Nonsmokers are quicker at remembering things than smokers. Research indicates smoking can affect your mental performance as much as a couple of drinks can.

The research on nicotine indicates that if you smoke, you shouldn't light up immediately before a memory task. Nor should you deprive yourself of a smoke for long hours prior to it because the privation will make you jittery and distract you from the task.

In general, you're better off not using stimulants. They may keep you awake, but they also make you more distractible—putting you at a disadvantage at memory tasks. If you need to fight fatigue, relatively safe stimulants like coffee or tea in moderation may be useful. But what helps most is a dose of motivation.

Attention!

Have you ever mumbled an automatic thank-you to a vending machine or stepped into the shower with your socks on? In these cases, concentration has failed you. Disrupted concentration impairs attention, which, of course, affects how much information you register and remember.

In your everyday life, you may find that you're unable to focus on what you're reading or on what others are saying. You may find that your concentration suffers when your emotions are stirred up—someone makes a snide remark at work, for instance, and you can't think about anything else.

You can't do much about rude remarks at work, but you can alter your daily routine to improve your concentration. A hectic and harried life-style can disorient people who are otherwise organized. Confusion hampers performance by lowering your level of attention and your ability to focus it. Anything you can do to slow your world down even a little bit will help your concentration and general memory skill.

Physical Condition Checklist

Clearly, good physical condition leads to good memory performance. To achieve your maximum memory performance, follow these guidelines:

• Promptly treat or seek treatment of major and minor illnesses. Discomfort distracts.

• Avoid alcohol, marijuana, coffee, and cigarettes. They may impair your ability to pay attention.

• Eat a well-balanced diet to ensure strength and optimal brain chemistry for memory tasks. And by eating moderately, you can avoid the sleepiness that often follows overeating.

• Get enough sleep and keep to your natural cycles of wakefulness and sleeping. This will keep you strong and alert enough to register and remember information.

• Take advantage of your peak times. If you can arrange it, schedule memory tasks for that time of day when you're at your best mentally, and most attentive.

• Rest regularly during the day when time allows, so you'll be up to your memory commitments.

• Stay in shape. Physical vigor is necessary for mental vigor, and physical weariness is always coupled with mental weariness.

Improving your ability to concentrate will be hampered if your life-style is too hectic. But a life that is too routine and too predictable can hamper your memory as well.

But don't slow it down *too* much. A very predictable and routine life-style can *also* lower your attention and ability to concentrate.

Think of a task you do very well. Most likely, you're so relaxed and adept at that task that you can do several other things at the same time. Proficiency is admirable and rewarding, of course, but sometimes it backfires. Research shows that when you have a great deal of experience at a task your performance sometimes becomes so automatic that you stop paying full attention to it. Errors increase as your attention wanders, and this can have serious consequences.

Your ability to concentrate is affected by how well your environment allows you to pay attention to what you're doing. In general, *slight* discomfort makes a person more alert and attentive than coziness does. Total comfort makes you feel safe, but it may also make you feel drowsy.

You wouldn't want to do your reading or learning on the sidewalk in midtown Manhattan during rush hour, but you probably wouldn't want to do it in total silence either. Ironically, the silence might be distracting. You'll probably be at your best if you perform your mental work while wearing comfortable clothes and sitting at comfortable furniture.

Whether your environment provides too little or too much comfort is a matter of personal taste. Some people work their best wearing a jacket and tie. If you truly function best with rock 'n' roll blasting in the background, then let it blast on. It would be a mistake to put on Bach or to turn the stereo off altogether.

Moods: The Good, the Bad, and the Ugly

Negative moods are known to impair memory performance. A slightly negative mood, such as the "down" you feel after a rough day, diminishes your ability to pay attention. An *intensely* negative mood, such as might occur after an argument with someone you care about, is even more debilitating. If the intense mood also involves anger or rage, you are likely to be too energized and distracted to perform memory tasks well, if at all.

Depression is a threat to memory. Normal depression actually alters brain chemistry in a way that slows absorption and emergence of information. In turn, this lowers your level of attention and reduces your capacity to focus attention.

Bad moods and depression will negatively affect your memory.

Severe depression (called *clinical depression*) weakens memory so much that some doctors see memory failure as a tip-off that a patient has a depression problem—even if the patient hasn't complained of depression. Treatments that relieve depression (antidepressant drugs and psychotherapy) usually have a positive effect on memory.

On the other hand, when things are going your way and you feel positive about life, your powers of attention soar and you perform memory tasks more efficiently. But just like comfort, too much of a good thing can be hurtful. When you're deliriously happy, such as when you fall in love or get a big promotion, you pay more attention to your deliciously positive feelings and not enough attention to less exciting everyday tasks. Memory performance goes down. (Of course, in these cases, it may be worth it.)

Memory performance may weaken as a new romance intensifies.

Earlier I mentioned how some people, in the face of unreliable evidence, believe recall can be improved if you use alcohol or marijuana when you're learning something and again when you have to remember it. The same state-dependent theory has been proposed for moods—if you're in a good mood when you study, you'll do better if you're in a good mood during the big exam. If you're in a bad mood when you study, it would be better to be in a bad mood again during the exam.

There is some evidence that this might be true. It's not clear, however, how to manipulate our moods to make them match up so carefully during our learning and remembering.

It is very difficult for humans to change a bad mood into a good mood deliberately. The best you can do is to turn your thoughts away from the things that put you in the bad mood and redirect them in a positive way.

Stress and Relaxation

People who report a lot of stress in their lives also report more memory failures. For example, studies show that nurses who work in hospital intensive care wards have more memory failures than those who work in routine wards. Stress can be an enemy to memory.

But once again, a little stress is better than none at all. Just as stage fright can cause an actor to forget a line, total complacency may cause him to miss a cue. Similarly, anxiety before a test will distract you and hamper your recall, but indifference to the importance of a test may make you take it too lightly and overlook important clues.

A proper level of stress keeps you alert and active as you cope with the challenges of everyday life. The trick is to see that your stress level doesn't get too· low or too high. Relaxation is one way to accomplish that.

Relaxation techniques will help you achieve the right stress level for optimum memory performance.

Some people relax by listening to music or watching television. Others prefer to jump out of airplanes or chop

The yoga position called the candle can help enhance memory.

up firewood with an ax. However you choose to achieve it, relaxation reduces stress, improves your mood, and decreases the distractibility that interferes with memory performance.

Perhaps the form of relaxation best known to facilitate memory is yoga. Hatha-yoga teaches a series of exercises or body *postures*. The movements are similar to those in traditional calisthenics, but are executed in slower and more graceful ways.

Yoga's effectiveness in producing a physiological state of relaxation—which is beneficial to memory—is widely accepted. Certain body postures, such as a headstand or a position called the candle (see page 55), are believed to be particularly beneficial to memory performance. Not everyone is able to do these, and some people shouldn't even try, especially if they have certain vascular, back, or neck problems. (Ask your doctor for an okay.) Simply lying on a bed and hanging your head down over the edge may be just as useful.

The idea is to get your head lower than the rest of your body. Driving more blood to the brain helps brain function in general and facilitates memory performance immediately following the exercise and long afterwards. This head inversion technique has been shown to improve the memory performance of older people who use it.

Yoga is helpful when it comes to boosting brain power.

Another group of yoga postures that may help memory involves the spine. These postures gently twist the spine, as you would when locking your knees while touching your toes with the opposite hand.

The yoga procedure for *muscle relaxation* is also held to facilitate memory: You lie on a firm surface and relax the muscles of your body one by one until your body is entirely flaccid. In this relaxed state, you can study (with a tape recorder, because lifting a book would disrupt the relaxation) or attempt to remember something you found hard to recall previously.

Researchers are convinced that regular muscle relaxation makes people less susceptible to stress-related illness and acts as an aid to memory (especially with elderly people). More research is needed to explore and validate all the various claims of hatha-yoga. But to the extent that the exercises help you relax, it can certainly provide some benefit to memory.

Yoga is not the only system of relaxation. Numerous others have appeared in the past two decades:

- Transcendental meditation (TM), perhaps the best known, in which you repeat a word or sound (called a mantra) to court physical and mental relaxation.
- Positive imaging, a method of creating and dwelling on comforting mental pictures and soothing fantasies.
- Sensory deprivation (the Lily tank), in which you float in a tank of body temperature water, shut off from all sight, sound, odor, allowing your mind to drift in a neutral state of utter relaxation.
- Alpha wave control, a system for learning to control your brain waves to induce calm and pleasant moods.
- Biofeedback, a way of learning to control your blood pressure and pulse rate to bring on serenity and relaxation.
- Neurolinguistic programming, a technique for controlling what you say to yourself so your internal messages remain positive and strengthening.

These are some of the most popular relaxation techniques, but new ones are being developed faster than researchers are able to test them. It's wise to use those that have been around a while. Properly used, the best systems can reduce stress and facilitate your memory performance in at least the short term.

Of course, no single relaxation system works for everybody. In fact, these tension-easing techniques can have just the opposite effect on some people—making them edgy instead of calming them down, causing depression instead of joy. If you do decide to undertake training in one of these systems, investigate to make sure that the one you choose is well suited to your personality and temperament. On the other hand, it's important to know that *you* may not need an organized program to help you relax. Stretching out on the sofa for a half hour, listening to your favorite music, reminiscing with friends, working out, or snorkeling—if that's your preference—may relax you sufficiently to achieve better memory performance.

A Better Attitude

Each of us has a particular *attitude* toward any memory situation that arises. Many people, for example, find the study of foreign languages a fascinating and personally rewarding experience. Others see such a pursuit as a big waste of time. Furthermore, the person who appreciates language study may willingly devote a lot of energy to learning French or Greek, but have no interest whatsoever in learning Russian or German.

Your attitude can help or hamper your memory performance. If you want to learn French and are excited by the task, most likely it will be much easier for you than for someone who is only studying the language to pass a course required for graduation. Your attitude affects how hard you try and your ability to sustain attention while performing memory tasks.

A bad attitude translates into a bad memory.

Because memory performance is affected by attitude, one way to improve your memory performance is to improve these attitudes. Typically, attitudes are deeply rooted. The origins of your attitudes lie in your upbringing and past experience. It's not easy to change them, but they can be changed.

Certain types of material are especially difficult to register and remember, not only because of the nature of the material but because of your attitude toward it.

Uninteresting Information

If you find something boring, it can be hard to register and remember. We often forget things simply because we weren't interested when the material was first presented, and we didn't pay attention.

The trick is to decide *ahead of time* which information you must remember and which is not important. Then, when you recognize something as uninteresting but important for you to know, take extra steps to ensure that you'll remember it. You must convince yourself that, although the material is a big snooze, you simply *have* to learn it.

If you're going to attend a dull lecture or business meeting that you sense may be important down the line, take extra care to get yourself mentally "up" for it. Reward yourself for hanging in there. Say to yourself, "If I can only make it through this next awful hour, I'll treat myself to _____."

Don't give in to your temptation to scoff at the material and do other work. Pay special attention to the speaker. Take careful notes. Try to think of ways you could make the same material more interesting. Convince yourself that while the experience may be unpleasant, some greater good will come of it. Establish a long-term goal, even if it's only that learning the material will make you a more well-rounded person. I could tell you 30 other ways to make material more interesting, but in the end it comes down to you. You have to convince yourself.

Taking notes during a lecture, meeting, or class that bores you can help you register information you would otherwise forget.

Negative Information

Memories connected with strong negative emotions are usually easy to remember. In fact, sometimes they're so easy to remember that we can't forget them no matter how hard we try.

But memories connected with only *moderately* negative emotions may be difficult to recall. The emotion can lead you to *suppress* the memory, which means to block it out of your mind. Suppression is a common reaction to negative feelings. Many people miss their dentist appointments, for instance, because the experience of going to the dentist is so unpleasant for them that they conveniently, but honestly, "forget" to go. As Scarlett O'Hara said, "I'll think about it tomorrow."

If you really don't want to do something, it's not surprising that your brain helps you forget to do it.

There are two ways to protect a memory against suppression. First, get yourself to view the negative information positively. Obviously, this is not always possible or appropriate. It's one thing to look on the bright side and convince yourself that a visit to the dentist may prevent future visits, but positive feelings are hard to come by if you get fired and have a family to support.

Another way to protect a memory against suppression is to *force* yourself to think about it. Say you must remember to attend a meeting where you'll be asked to discuss that bungled project you were responsible for. The best approach would be to make a note about the meeting in your appointment book and ask someone to give you a timely reminder, then set two alarms, two hours and one hour before the meeting. Review the details of the project before going in. Make a special effort to be knowledgeable about what went wrong. Show everyone that you learned something from the experience by figuring out how you can prevent such a disaster from occurring again. Demonstrate how this can help them all and show that you came away a better person.

It takes a special effort to overcome suppressed memories.

Suppression is mentally running away from problems. If you take deliberate steps to *face up* to negative memories, suppression is less likely to occur.

Personally Upsetting Information

It's a familiar soap opera cliché: A character suffers a bad experience and is so traumatized that he or she doesn't remember it at all. Some negative memories are so threatening that we *repress* them. While suppressed memories can be remembered with some effort, repressed memories cannot be remembered at will. Repression removes any awareness of the information from our conscious memory.

Many psychologists believe that we all repress memories to a degree, but for some people it becomes a serious problem. Access to repressed memories comes only after recalling many related memories (Freud called the process psychoanalysis). If you suspect that you are repressing part or all of important memories and it is interfering with your happiness, consult a clinical psychologist about the problem. The recovery of repressed memories is something we cannot expect to do ourselves.

Sometimes, memories are not suppressed *or* repressed—they are distorted. For instance, you may have a terrible job interview or awful first date and convince yourself that things didn't go as badly as they really did. Or you may have a *terrific* experience and somehow convince yourself that it was a disaster. Memories tend to act as revisionist historians.

Self-distortions are difficult to detect because they protect our self-image. We want our memories to be consistent with our self-image and goals. An optimistic person might "edit" memories to make them more positive, while a person with low self-esteem might make things out to be worse than they really were.

Our memories are consistent with our self-image and our goals.

Our friends and loved ones are often the first to recognize and point out that we are distorting reality. By being open to the possibility, we are more likely to discover and correct these memories. Some distortion is normal, but an excessive amount can lead to maladjustment.

Get Real

Having a good attitude is good and having a bad attitude is bad, right? Well, not necessarily. If you *think* that you're simply fantastic at remembering appointments, for instance, you may be inclined to do that task in your head. A person who *does not think* he is very good at remembering appointments is likely to make a note of them. If the two of you schedule a meeting, he may show up and you may forget about it.

Positive attitudes that are unrealistic will only lead us astray, making us try tasks we should avoid or put too little effort into tasks we incorrectly suppose we do well.

On the other hand, you may have a negative attitude about performing a certain memory task that you know you're good at. Many good students dislike the process of studying. Their attitude may lead them to pay less attention as they study and to respond less quickly and efficiently while taking exams.

The goal is not to make your attitudes about memory tasks good or bad—but to make them *realistic*. If a certain memory task is genuinely simple for you, there's no point in devoting too much mental energy to it. If it's difficult but important, put in the effort needed to master it. If it's simply out of your league or not important to your life, don't waste your time on it. What you do need are *correct* attitudes so you do the tasks you're good at and work to become better at them, and avoid the tasks you find difficult.

If your efforts to improve your memory are faltering, give your attitude a reality check.

The diary and questionnaire of the previous chapter can serve as a "reality check" for your memory attitudes. Did you find that your answers on the questionnaire match up well with the results of keeping the diary for a month? If so, it indicates that your attitudes about performing memory tasks are realistic.

If the diary contradicts your answers on the questionnaire in some places, it suggests that the attitudes you held while taking the test were not correct and should be changed to match reality. You can improve your handling of memory tasks by correcting inappropriate attitudes.

Attention Training

All the things I've been talking about in this chapter—getting physically fit, eating right, relaxing, and such—will help improve your memory performance because they improve your capacity to pay attention. The only drawback is that these improvements are temporary. If you can't find time to squeeze in your regular relaxation period, for instance, any benefits you get out of it will disappear.

What we need, then, are training techniques that will produce a *permanent* increase in our capacity for attention. Research indicates that adults *can* improve their ability at *particular* tasks. If you want to improve your attention skills, you should practice in situations that are very similar to the ones in which you want your memory to succeed.

For example, suppose you find it difficult to pay attention to a speaker during a meeting or lecture. You could work on this problem by renting "how-to" videotapes that feature people simply presenting information, as in a lecture. Practice focusing all your attention on what the person is saying. There's no pressure because there are no negative consequences for failure in this situation. Under these circumstances, you may find that the benefits of the practice will transfer over to real-life meetings and lectures.

Try these basic informal attention training techniques at home on your own:

Increase your ability to sustain your attention. Have you ever played the license plate game on a long automobile trip? It's simple: Make a list of all 50 states and try to see if the family can spot a license plate from each one.

Anything that forces you to take note of an infrequent sight or sound should help you increase your attention span. Sentries in the military, police officers on a stakeout, and security guards train themselves to detect the slightest noise that might indicate an intruder. You don't have to stake out your neighbors, but you can practice listening for faint, unpredictable sounds or looking for dim lights in total darkness. Watch and listen for planes in the sky, for instance.

Anything that forces you to take note of an infrequent sight or sound helps you increase your ability to pay attention.

Increase your ability to divide your attention. When Lyndon Johnson was president, he used to watch the evening news on three television sets at the same time, each one tuned to a different channel. Later, he was able to remember how each network covered the news. I have heard that there are game show fans who do this all the time.

This is an easy and intriguing way to practice dividing your attention. Put two TV sets next to one another, tune them to different channels, and try to absorb as much information from each as possible. You'll notice your attention drifting from one to another, depending on the programs. With some practice your concentration will improve. Eventually, you may carry this skill over to following the swirl of conversation better the next time you attend a noisy party.

Learn how to divide your attention effectively.

Increase your ability to notice details. The next time you have a new experience—going to a new restaurant, for instance—make a special effort to really drink it in. How is the place decorated? How many tables are in the room? How old does your waiter appear to be? Instead of just diving into the menu, make it a point to pick out the details of your surroundings.

By going out of your way to observe your world, you can sharpen your ability to notice details in the future. Pretend you're a detective looking for murder clues. Or put on a long selection of music and listen for one particular instrument throughout. When driving, try to notice street signs. Go to the movies and study the whole image, not just the characters who are speaking.

Increase your ability to resist distraction. Turn on those two television sets to different channels again. This

---

You can learn how to resist distraction if you practice listening to one TV while ignoring another playing in the same room.

---

time, instead of trying to absorb *everything*, concentrate on one program and try to ignore the other. As you get better at concentrating your attention, turn the volume lower on the TV you're attending to, and higher on the distracting TV.

Mental Condition Checklist

A good mental condition is necessary for good memory performance. To be at your sharpest, follow these guidelines:

• Avoid both a hectic lifestyle and getting into a rut. Too little or too much to do lessens your capacity to pay attention.

• Keep stress at a manageable level. A little stress keeps you alive and alert to perform memory tasks, but too much of it makes you distractible.

• Relax a little bit every day. Take an occasional vacation or weekend off to renew your strength. Take a catnap when necessary to recharge your batteries and just before having to do a memory task. Try innovative ways of relaxing, such as yoga exercise and meditation.

• Exercise. You'll be less stressed, stronger, and have a more positive viewpoint when you perform memory tasks.

• Talk out your problems. A more positive outlook will help you to register and remember better.

• Choose a harmonious environment for learning. Discomfort cuts into your concentration for studying; too much comfort may make you drowsy.

• Maintain realistic attitudes towards memory tasks.

Summary

If you have a big test or meeting coming up, you know you can prepare for it. But the only way to ensure improved performance of memory tasks that you either can't see coming or don't recognize until they have come and gone is to work to improve your physical and mental condition.

By doing this, you make yourself ready to pay attention to memory tasks and make your long-term memory ready to absorb new memories (traces) or have old traces emerge.

Chapter 5

MEET THE PEOPLE: YOUR MEMORY ON STAGE

If you think it's tough to memorize facts and figures when you're alone, I have a little bad news for you. Your memory is even more likely to fail in the company of others. Social factors can have a strong negative effect on memory performance.

Every social situation requires you to demonstrate your memory. When you see an acquaintance or business associate, you have to recall dozens of facts about that person. You may have to remember that you were supposed to get together, return a favor, repay a loan, or complete a task for the other person.

In essence, social situations are *performances* in which your memory takes center stage. And your ability to remember often determines how others judge you. If you remember that Mr. Jones's daughter was recently accepted into medical school, he'll appreciate it; he'll think even more of you if you bring it up in conversation. If you forget that he even *has* a daughter, he'll probably assume that you care nothing about him personally, or worse—that you are simply stupid. So you see how readily social relationships can be affected by your ability to recall.

Social settings may be enjoyable but they really give your brain a workout.

There are so many ways for your memory to fail in the company of others. Sometimes you simply don't realize that you're expected to commit something to memory, or perhaps the social situation—such as a cocktail party—is too distracting to allow you to use your memory to the max. On still other occasions, you learn and remember information perfectly, but fail to communicate it clearly to the people around you.

In this chapter, we'll look at memory in a social context. You'll learn how to train your mind to react correctly—even impressively—when around other people, especially when your recall isn't working 100 percent.

Taking Mental Notes

How often have you been greeted enthusiastically by someone but you can't, for the life of you, remember who the person is? In such a case, you can only search for conversational clues that might disclose who this person is and where you met before.

But if you had spotted the same person across a large room, you would have had time to figure it out: Did I go to school with him? Did we play on the same team? By the time he got close enough to shake your hand, perhaps you would have remembered who he was so you could greet him appropriately.

Social etiquette requires you to be a virtual memory wizard every day. For example, you step out of your house and you see the Arbuckle family from down the street closing in on you. Mrs. Arbuckle expects that you'll remember to ask about her new baby. Mr. Arbuckle always talks politics, so you'd better come up with something about the latest government scandal lest you appear uninformed. The Arbuckle's son is tagging along and his parents will expect you to recall that he did well in a recent science fair at school. But you're struggling just to remember his *name*.

If you're suddenly thrust into a situation like this, responding quickly and correctly can be tough. But if you're prepared ahead of time, your chances of successful recall increase significantly. Train your mind to get ready for upcoming situations in which you'll be expected to remember things about people. You'll perform these tasks more efficiently and accurately if you do.

Train your mind to be prepared for situations in which you'll be expected to remember things about people.

When you see the Arbuckles coming down the street, take the very sight of them as a sign that the curtain is going up on another memory performance. Pause a moment to anticipate the likely topics of conversation. What do you have in common with these people? What is important to them? What was discussed the last time you got together? This pause gives your memory the chance to call up relevant information and have it ready when you meet them face-to-face.

Similarly, when you first meet a person you expect to see again, make a conscious effort to take mental notes about him or her. Study the face and features. Look for a physical characteristic that stands out and try to remember it. Select a few of the main points you discussed and file them away for future reference.

For instance, your mental notes after a first meeting with someone might read: *Joe Burns—beard—architect—went to school with my sister in Oregon.*

The next time you meet Joe Burns, you'll be armed with this information. You'll pick up your conversation and learn more about Joe. Gradually, if you see Joe frequently, your profile of him will become so rich that you won't need mental tricks anymore. Memory regarding Joe will be automatic, just as it is when you see your family and close friends.

Social Events: Memory in Overdrive

Receptions, meetings, reunions, and other get-togethers require that you remember many pieces of information before you arrive. You need to know how to dress, what to bring, and when you're expected to show up. Once you arrive, you'll need to remember a variety of names, topics, and protocols.

Imagine that the party will include several people you don't know. You'll probably be introduced to them shortly after you walk in the door, and it's likely you'll be told a few facts about each person. You'll make small talk for a few minutes and then move on to the next person. In the meantime, other guests you already know may greet you.

Minutes or hours later, you'll inevitably bump into one of the people you were introduced to earlier. This is the tough part. You want to recall the person's name at least, and hopefully a few facts about him or her. Then, before you leave the gathering, you must remember to thank the host and tell your new acquaintances how nice it was to meet them.

Such engagements might well be regarded as *memory rituals*. They demand continual registration and remembering of both old and new information. And if you play a starring role in the event (your own wedding, for example), we're talking about a massive amount of information. Your power to recall is on public display even more at a testimonial, roast, eulogy, religious ceremony, or the like, where you must use a memorized text.

Memory preparation will really help make these situations easier. As soon as you receive an invitation to a social event, take stock right then and there of the memory tasks you'll face. Besides the details of place, time, and purpose, consider the likely topics of conversation. Think about the people you might meet and why they might be there. Ask yourself what they're likely to discuss that you'll be expected to remember. If possible, go over the guest list. It provides an opportunity to anticipate the interests of those attending and plan some easy conversation starters.

At the actual event, when you are introduced to the first new person, it's important *at that instant* to rehearse mentally what you just learned about the person. So many people let their eyes glaze over in situations like this. They shake hands and exchange pleasantries with strangers, but never register who it is they just met. Ten seconds later, they can't come up with the name.

Introductions require you to imprint a person's name in your memory at that instance.

If that describes you, it doesn't mean you have a bad memory for names or faces. It probably means that you're somewhat overwhelmed in these social situations and your memory system shuts down. You can overcome this problem by mentally recording a few facts about each person you meet and making a special effort to rehearse this information in your mind several times before moving on to the next new face.

Let's Get Personal

Certain memory situations symbolize good relationships and convey affection, respect, and love for the people who are close to you. Forgetting what your Aunt Betty's favorite food is may seem trivial to you, but if it's important to her, your faulty memory might damage your entire relationship. When you recognize that remembering a certain piece of information acts as a symbol of your feelings to someone else, take extra care to make special note of its importance. Of course, you can't remember the birthday, anniversary, and details in the life of everybody you know, but close friends and loved ones deserve your special attention. (Many people keep a "birthday calendar" reserved for noting these special events.)

What you remember about people is a symbol of your feelings toward them.

Here are some basics for personal remembering:

- The person's full name and its proper spelling, of course, plus title, and career history, especially successes.
- Promises you made—and whether you kept them.
- Special events you shared.
- Likes, dislikes, pet causes, and hobbies.
- Appointments to keep.
- The routines you share (a special greeting or parting kiss, a favorite dessert you like to split, buying a particular flower for a meaningful anniversary).
- Special occasions to be honored (birthday and anniversary, Valentine's Day, Mother's Day, Secretary's Week, and such).
- Tasks expected of you and considered important.
- Mannerisms you recognize that indicate approval, disapproval, a need for action, a change in the person's mood.
- Areas of the person's expertise, and the need to show deference when these topics arise.

The best way to remember information about the key people in your life is to make a list of those things each person might regard as important in your relationship.

Once you establish this list, consider situations that might require you to perform specific tasks for that person.

Write down interesting information you learn about people. Then rehearse it from time to time to keep the facts straight in your memory.

As you mow the lawn or travel to work, mentally review your list. Such "mindless" tasks afford a wonderful opportunity to improve your memory. When you rehearse learned information mentally, memory is strengthened. So instead of letting your thoughts wander aimlessly as you mow or drive, use the time to reinforce the information you want to retain.

Memory Pacts: "You Wash, I'll Dry"

Sometimes we make what I call *memory pacts* with people. You know what I mean: "You remember to take out the trash, and I'll remember to stop for milk on the way home." "You remember to keep an eye on the Wallace account, and I'll handle the Toporik account." "You wash, I'll dry." These pacts are especially common among people who live or work together.

Often, memory pacts are made without a word being spoken. Naturally, when communication isn't clear, one or both parties may fail to keep their part of the bargain. How many husbands and wives have argued over who was supposed to be paying attention when the nice man was giving directions at the side of the road? ("I thought *you* were listening!")

Memory pacts can cause friction in relationships if intentions are not clearly communicated.

Most of us can't recall all of our memory pacts at will, but we do recognize each one as it comes up, especially when it's broken. Pacts are intentions and, like any intention, can be easily forgotten. Try to make at least a mental note when you realize that you've entered into a memory pact with someone. And if you can communicate the pact to the other person clearly, you'll minimize the chance that either of you will forget your mutual memory task.

Your Memory Reputation

We've all had the experience of thinking we remembered something accurately, only to be told by someone else that we had it all wrong.

Each of us has his or her own idea of what constitutes a good memory performance. It's not enough that *you* know your memory is correct. If someone else erroneously thinks his memory is richer and more accurate, he's not likely to defer to yours. Sometimes a friend may have no idea what happened during a particular event, but still he refuses to accept your recollection of it. This can be infuriating.

Fairly or unfairly, other things besides accuracy influence how other people judge your memory. Probably most important is your "memory reputation." If you are involved with any group of people long enough, you acquire a reputation for having a good memory or a bad one. Like reputations for other personality characteristics (loyalty, diligence, discretion), the one for memory is generally based on past behavior patterns.

Your friends' reactions to your memory failure depend on your memory reputation. If people think of you as having a terrific memory, they excuse you willingly when you do forget something—you were tired, even the best falter sometimes. But if you're known to have a bad memory and you make the very same mistake, people tend to think you're incompetent and hold it against you. If, in spite of your reputation for a bad memory, you should remember some obscure fact, the triumph may be labeled as a fluke.

A bad memory can make you appear incompetent. Take the steps needed to improve your memory's accuracy.

There's an analogy in the sports world. When a superstar like Brooks Robinson fumbled a ball at third base, it was excused as a rare mistake. But if Joe Shmoe were to make a similar error, it would be further proof of Joe's lousy fielding. And if poor Joe were to make a spectacular play, the guys in the bleachers would say he got lucky. If you have a bad reputation, you can't win.

The only way to change a bad memory reputation into a good one is to demonstrate convincingly and consistently that your recollection of events and facts is accurate.

Here's how:

- Take responsibility for learning and remembering correctly any information you should know in your role as a relative, a friend, an employee, and as a citizen. (Your memory in this area—good or bad—is bound to show itself sooner or later, so take the opportunity to firm up your reputation for having a reliable memory.)
- Make it a matter of honor to do what you say you will do. (Perform these deeds at first opportunity while they're fresh in your mind; mentally reconstruct conversations that might involve a commitment on your part; make a note about a promise not yet fulfilled; and don't agree to do anything you can't do or don't intend to do.)
- Volunteer pertinent information when you know you're right, provided the situation permits you to do so without appearing bombastic or patronizing, and invite others to expand on your statement.
- Never volunteer information unless you're absolutely certain that it's accurate.
- If you are invited to contribute information, admit to any uncertainty you have about it before giving your recollection of an experience or a point of fact.

Memory Stereotypes

Some people might mistrust your memory because of cultural stereotypes about memory. This phenomenon was borne out several years ago in an experiment I conducted with my students at Hamilton College in New York state. The students were asked to rate a list of various types of people on four kinds of memory ability, from superior to inferior. See the accompanying list for the results.

Note that the ratings are on a scale of 1 to 7, where 1 is an inferior memory and 7 is a superior memory.

Memory Power by Stereotypes

Subject	Knowledge (objective facts)	Events (personal experiences)	Intentions (follow-through)	Actions (skills)	Average
Family					
Young adult	4.4	4.8	4.5	4.5	4.6
Wife	4.6	5.1	4.7	4.0	4.6
Husband	4.8	4.8	4.0	4.4	4.5
Middle-aged person	5.1	4.7	4.1	4.2	4.5
Senior citizen	4.6	4.2	3.4	3.5	3.9
Child	2.5	3.4	3.5	3.5	3.2
Occupation					
Airline pilot	6.0	5.1	5.8	6.4	5.8
Lawyer	6.6	5.4	5.1	5.1	5.6
Professor	6.9	5.2	4.8	4.5	5.4
Mechanic	5.2	4.0	5.0	6.4	5.2
Reporter	5.4	5.8	4.9	4.7	5.2
Receptionist	4.9	4.9	5.3	5.0	5.0
Politician	5.9	5.3	4.8	4.1	5.0
Police officer	4.9	4.5	5.0	5.7	5.0
Plumber	4.7	3.8	5.0	5.8	4.8
Company spokesperson	5.5	4.5	4.7	4.1	4.7
Salesperson	5.3	4.4	4.4	4.3	4.6

Notice how the overall ratings (averages of the four categories) are lowest for a child, highest for young and middle-aged adults, and lower again for senior citizens. Among the occupations, airline pilots were judged to have the best memory over all, although lawyers and professors were judged higher when it came to knowledge.

A person's occupation may suggest the level of memory ability.

Obviously, people are ready to rate your memory as good or poor without even meeting you. The students who made these ratings had neither the training nor the opportunity to make an informed assessment of these different kinds of people. Their ratings were based entirely on stereotypes that we all pick up in our culture. It follows that we're likely to be judged by others in the same way. So when someone refuses to accept your recollection of an event, keep in mind that it may be due to a stereotype associated with your age, occupation, gender, race, or some other characteristic.

Such time-honored mind-sets are virtually impossible to change. But you can take steps to alter what people think about you personally. If your memory is viewed by some as unrealistically accurate and that pressures you to perform, you may want to *relax* when demonstrating your memory in their company—you're already doing very well in their eyes. If your memory is viewed by others as unrealistically poor, make a *greater* effort to prepare for memory tasks, in an effort to correct their unfair negative bias.

Head Games

For the most part, when you're judged on the basis of a memory stereotype or memory reputation, no harm is intended. But sometimes people *contrive* to make your memory performance appear better or worse than it is to further their own social goals. Their comments about your memory may be intended to flatter or insult you, or they may be intended to show you kindness or anger indirectly. In either case, there's an ulterior motive lurking in there, and you should watch for it.

These memory head games are especially common:

Memory insult. Someone points out a memory failure on your part that might have been overlooked otherwise, noting the incident as indicative of your "bad memory."

For example, suppose you forget that Columbus's third ship was the Santa Marìa. A companion criticizes you for your stupidity.

Chances are that the person who does this is angry with you for something unrelated to his love of history.

Memory praise. Someone praises your success at a memory task far in terms beyond what it deserves and claims this is indicative of your "good memory."

You can detect ulterior motives in a person's insults or praise.

For example, you remember the Niña, Pinta, and Santa Marìa, and a companion declares you to be a genius!

Enjoy the praise, but beware that the other person might want something from you.

Memory alibi. Someone makes excuses for a memory failure you have.

For example, suppose you forget to pick up the laundry on the way home from work. Your companion forgives this mistake, noting that after a long day you have a right to be tired.

Perhaps, but the comment may be based on a desire to get a favor from you later.

Memory responsibility charge. Someone claims that performing a memory task was your responsibility and not his own.

For example, you arrive home without the laundry, thinking that your companion was supposed to pick it up, only to be accused of being irresponsible.

Your companion does not want to accept responsibility for something that went wrong, preferring to pass the buck.

Memory noncooperation. Someone fails to help you at a memory task, although he or she is quite capable of doing so.

For example, in response to a question, you say, "The Niña, The Pinta, and. . . and. . ." but you just can't get it. A friend, who surely knows the answer, volunteers nothing.

Such an obvious decision not to help could be an indication that your friend may not be such a good friend after all or is angry at you for some reason and is enjoying your little struggle.

Memory fraud. Someone claims your memory is in error on some point, although you both know that this claim is untrue.

For example, a companion insists emphatically that Columbus sailed the ocean blue in 1497.

This person is playing with you for his own personal amusement. Such an obvious distortion bodes ill for your relationship with this person.

If someone makes a negative and untrue remark about your memory and you believe it, your confidence may drop and a future memory failure may result. Unrealistically positive remarks may give you an inflated sense of your memory ability and cause you to stop trying.

Some people also play head games with their *own* memory. Have you ever met someone who is constantly apologizing for supposed failures, often before they even occur? He might do this because he thinks it will make you feel superior in his presence and you will like him more as a result.

Watch out for those who might play a head game with your memory or their own. Examine the social motives that might be behind their statements. It's important to distinguish warped feedback from accurate and deserved feedback.

Trust Your Own Recall

The point that I've been driving toward is that memory seems to be such a fragile and insecure thing that we almost prefer to rely on the recollection of others than to trust our own.

In a recent experiment, a group of people were shown photographs of automobile accidents. When quizzed later, they were fairly good at remembering details in the photographs. A second group was shown the same photographs and then put in a room with people who had been instructed to give deliberately *false* information about the pictures. The second group, instead of relying on their own memory, tended to go along with what the bogus group said about the photographs.

Never rely on someone else's memory. Learn to trust your own.

Most people choose to disbelieve their own eyes— even if they're initially sure of their recollection—and accept the contradictory account other people give. We find it difficult to stick with a memory that differs from that of the crowd, especially if the crowd consists of well-respected friends or authorities. When you reminisce about the good old days with your friends, you may notice that you tend to doubt your recall and even revise your memory to line up with others who remember a story differently.

The accuracy of your recall can be affected by people who aren't even around! Considerable evidence shows that we mentally "edit" our memories to put what we've done or said into a more favorable social light. We tend to remember more about things that match up with our religious, political, and social beliefs and interests. If people are asked to read a perfectly balanced passage that discusses the pros and cons of a political issue, they're likely to remember the facts about the side they favor, and recall less about the position they oppose.

We tend to edit our memories to suit our own personal desires or beliefs.

To avoid having biased memories, spend extra time studying facts that stand *contrary* to your own position. Pay special attention to the points you oppose, because they are the ones you're most likely to forget. Not only will this help your recall, but people with opposing views will give you credit for being open-minded—because you possess an unusually accurate memory of points with which you don't agree.

There's no simple way to insulate your memory from the influence of social pressures. But bear in mind that your memory may very well be right when others say it's wrong. Guard against revising your memories just because someone challenges them. If others attack your recall of something, do a little research to see who is really right. If it turns out that you had it right all along, it will give you confidence when you encounter similar arguments in the future.

In general, you should be wary of using another person as the standard for judging your memory ability.

Don't automatically take the feedback you receive about your memory at face value. You're best off if your own attitudes about your memory abilities are accurate.

Using Your Friends as Paper and Pencil

Don't use someone else's memory as a replacement for your own. Don't make other people do your memory work for you. You've probably heard it a million times: "Honey, remind me to *(fill in the blank)* tomorrow."

Sometimes you don't feel like making the effort to remember something, and you ask someone to remember it for you. Maybe you ask them to answer a question you could handle yourself if you really tried. Or you ask them to remember a piece of information and to fill you in later.

Don't use other people as your paper and pencil. For one thing, the person you regard as a memory whiz may have a memory that's even worse than yours. But even if the person can be counted on to remember things for you, there's no such thing as a free lunch. People who are willing to remember for you expect to be paid back in some way. You have imposed on them and they know it.

Never ask others to do your remembering for you.

Furthermore, it's unfair to burden a friend with memory tasks you don't want to bother with yourself. It's best not to ask people to do your remembering for you, and to politely turn down requests to do it for others.

Communicating What You Remember

It doesn't matter how much you remember about something if you can't convince others that your recall is accurate. When that happens, it's not your memory that needs improvement, but your communication skills.

First off, memory claims have to be consistent to be convincing. If you tell somebody you were in Houston over New Year's Eve and a few minutes later you mention that you were in Bombay on January 1, almost *anything* you say from that point on will be discounted. Inconsistencies do appear, even in otherwise accurate recollections, but major contradictions of fact make the speaker seem confused and foolish.

In recalling a past event, strive to make the contents of your recall include only the most *essential* details. If you talk off the top of your head without thinking, you may stumble into inconsistencies without realizing it.

People are more likely to accept your recollections if you can back them up. A corroborating source, such as newspapers, books, or memos, will put more teeth into your reputation for a good memory. If someone remembers the event the same way you do, all the better—the more witnesses, the stronger the argument.

If you feel sure you remember something accurately, say so with confidence. John Dean, special counsel to President Nixon (1970–1973) and well-known whistle-blower in the Watergate scandal, was regarded as having an excellent memory because he conveyed his recall of the Nixon presidency in a convincing fashion. As it turned out, later investigation showed that Dean's recall, though substantially correct, had many inaccuracies. But he *made* people believe him by sitting up and speaking with confidence in his voice.

Communicating with confidence and skill goes a long way in improving your credibility.

When you describe something to other people from your memory, talk clearly, slowly, and at an even pace. Don't roll your eyes, scratch your head, or stare at the ceiling. Such traditional symbols of grasping for a memory are interpreted that way by an audience.

Be confident about what you remember, but be careful not to overstate your confidence or you'll be seen as blustering. That's also likely to hurt your credibility.

Speaking Your Mind

Most of us tend to think we either remember something or we don't remember it, with no in-between. Actually, we generally remember an event with varying degrees of certainty. If we have a very vague memory of it, we *suspect* our version is correct. If we feel a little more sure of our recall, we may *believe* or *think* it is accurate. If we're quite certain about the event, we *know*, *guarantee*, or even *swear* that something we remember is true.

No one has a perfect memory. Most of us remember with varying degrees of certainty.

Different memory terms have subtly different meanings. Your statement of recall is more credible when you couch it in language that expresses the right degree of certainty. Use this list of some common memory vocabulary to communicate your memory claims clearly:

Register—Commit to memory, load in memory, store in memory, make a mental note, imprint, learn, engrave in memory, learn by heart, memorize, enshrine in memory, burden the memory.

Retain—Preserve in memory, know by heart, know by rote, know without notes, know verbatim, fresh in memory, alive in memory, vivid in memory, uppermost in your thoughts, unable to get something out of your head, have at one's fingertips, hazy memory, cobwebs in the brain, pent-up memory, blocked memory, amnesia, lost in memory, buried in memory, treasure the memory, keep the memory alive.

Remember—Recall, call to mind, recollect, retrace, conjure up, dredge up, retrospect, rake up the past, reminisce, search the memory, recognize, acknowledge, recur to mind, flashback, cue, clue, fan the embers, prompt the memory, jog the memory, remind, bring back to memory.

Here are some classic types of rememberers—and forgetters—and their traits:

The normal rememberer—Good memory, retentive.

The exceptional rememberer—Photographic memory, memory like a tape recorder, memory like an encyclopedia.

The forgetter who does not pay attention—Absent-minded, thoughtless, careless, inattentive, oblivious, dim-witted, faulty memory, scatterbrained.

The forgetter who is mentally fatigued—Taxed memory, overloaded memory, dead memory.

The forgetter who has a defective memory—Forgetful, bad memory, failing memory, loose memory, memory like a sieve, brain has a short circuit, memory like a revolving door, poor short-term memory, poor long-term memory.

If you become more sensitive to the terminology of memory, you will express yourself better and others will be more likely to believe what you say. For example, when you forget to do something for a friend, you might choose to excuse yourself by saying your memory was "overloaded." The success of this claim, of course, will depend on whether you can also demonstrate *why* it was overloaded.

Couching your language in the right words will help to protect your reputation for having good memory skills.

Reading Minds through Body Language

When you walk down the street and see someone you recognize as a friend, a curious thing happens. The corners of your mouth turn up into a smile, the pupils in your eyes dilate, and your eyebrows arch upward. If the other person recognizes you, he or she will do the same.

These spontaneous signs show anyone watching that your mind is homing in on a piece of information. Like all of us, you demonstrate this process in a physical way at least a dozen times a day—scratching your head, knitting your brow, snapping your fingers as you try to recall— without realizing it. But you can use these same signs, deliberately, to your advantage.

Besides using the appropriate memory language, you can improve your communication skills *even more* by using signals effectively. If you definitely remember a piece of information but have a difficult time bringing it to mind and need a moment longer to think, you can repeatedly mutter "Oh..." or shake your hand in the air. If you're thinking, you can adopt a pensive look or a faraway stare.

Your body language can be a tip-off to others about how sure you are of yourself when it comes to recalling information.

Combining the right signals with verbal claims can make for a more persuasive case that your memory is accurate. The following signals concerning memory are virtually universal:

Forgetting—Blank stare, look of surprise, look of guilt, groans, profanity, facial twitch, rolling eyes.

Rules of Memory Etiquette

You won't hear about it from Emily Post or Miss Manners, but there is an unwritten social code of memory etiquette. Here is the unwritten code—written:

• Don't comment on another person's lack of memory ability. For example, if you point out that someone continually forgets items that were just mentioned, you appear rude.

• Ignore unimportant memory errors, especially if the person making the errors is a loved one.

• If someone starts to tell you a story that he or she told you before, grin and bear it—especially if that person is elderly. And when Grandpa goes into the Battle of Guadalcanal for the 200th time, consider that someday you'll be repeating tales of your own just as he does.

• If the situation demands that you correct someone else's memory error, do it in a nice way. Instead of asserting, "Tuesday is wrong. It's supposed to be Friday," it's better to couch your correction in terms of a reminder, "You meant Friday, didn't you?"

• When your conversation is interrupted for whatever reason, make the effort to register what was being discussed before the interruption. When you don't remember what someone was just talking about, you appear uninterested and insincere.

• Remember another person's successes and ignore his or her failures.

Trying to remember—Thinker's pose, faraway stare, upward or downward stare, pensive look, scratching the head, hitting forehead with palm, adjusting posture.

"Tip-of-the-tongue" state—Snapping the fingers, shaking the fist, repeated "oh's."

Summary

The key to success at memory tasks involving other people is to prepare in advance.

Forgetting is often seen as symbolic of your disregard for someone. Be aware of memory pacts you have made with others.

Be conscious of your memory reputation and any memory stereotypes that apply to you.

Don't revise what you remember simply because someone challenges your recollection.

Don't ask other people to remember things for you.

Express your recollections confidently, consistently, using appropriate memory language and nonverbal signals.

Chapter 6

MENTAL MANIPULATIONS

Ever since the days of the ancient Greeks, memory experts have tried to devise simple mental tricks to help people overcome the limitations of memory. I call these techniques *mental manipulations.*

Here's an example of a mental manipulation you've probably used yourself without any formal memory training:

You want to order a pizza, so you look up a number in the telephone book, say, 769-3268. Instead of jotting it down on paper, you make a dash to the phone, repeating to yourself the whole time: 7693268. . . 7693268. . . 7693268. Quickly you dial the number.

By the time the person at the pizza parlor picks up the phone, you probably don't remember the number anymore. But your mental manipulation served its short-term purpose perfectly, and you would not have remembered those seven digits without it.

By using mental manipulations properly, you can improve your memory in certain situations 100 to 200 percent. Many formal studies at many universities have shown this. Typically, subjects are given a 30-item list and asked to memorize as many items as possible within a limited time period. Those who receive no training in mental manipulations remember an average of 10 items. The people who learn certain mental manipulations remember about 20 items (a 100 percent increase). Finally, those trained in *other* mental manipulations are able to learn all 30 items on the list (a 200 percent increase).

Learning and using mental manipulations can improve your memory 200 percent.

Mental manipulations work, and the more of them you use, the better your memory is.

Which Mental Manipulations Should You Use?

It would be nice if you could learn just a single mental manipulation and use it across the board for all memory situations. Unfortunately, memory isn't that simple. Research shows that you can't improve your overall memory substantially without mastering a broad assortment of techniques.

This chapter will introduce you to a wide variety of mental manipulations. Some were devised centuries ago, others in the late 1980s. Some emphasize rehearsal, such as the way you remembered the pizza parlor's phone number; others work by embellishing information or forming associations. My goal is to help you prepare for all kinds of situations, especially unexpected memory tasks.

Even someone with an incredible memory couldn't learn all the mental manipulations in this book. The trick is to choose the manipulations that suit you. Let your intellectual style and tastes determine which ones you learn. There's no sense in trying to learn a technique that seems foreign, weird, or silly to you.

The mind tricks you choose to learn should reflect your personality and interests.

As you go through this chapter, consider these questions as you select manipulations:

- Do you like to live simply? Then choose simple manipulations.
- Do you like intricate stories and explanations? Then choose manipulations that have complexity.
- Do you like crossword puzzles and creative use of language? Go for the verbal manipulations: Many of them are like word games.
- Do you like to imagine scenes from your past and enjoy conjuring up images? The imagery-based manipulations may be especially useful to you. But if you have trouble visualizing images, avoid the manipulations that call for imagery.
- Do you enjoy imagining sounds and rhythms? If you do, try manipulations that emphasize acoustic imagery.

Of course, the best way to find out if a manipulation will help you remember is to try using it. Compare the effort and effectiveness of different manipulations. Generally the best manipulation meets your goals for effectiveness and fits your intellectual style as well. Out of the many techniques presented in the following pages, you're sure to find some that you can adapt to your own needs and abilities.

How Do These Techniques Work?

Mental manipulations intensify your attention during the learning, retention, and retrieval phases of the memory process. This in turn influences what you absorb into long-term memory. It happens in four distinct ways:

Learning to master certain mind manipulations will also help you grow intellectually.

---

1. *Strength.* Some of the mental manipulations that you're going to read about serve to increase the strength of a memory trace. When you repeated the phone number of that pizza parlor to yourself, you were boosting the strength of the information in order to keep it in your working memory longer. Similarly, if you were to look at a photograph in bright light, you would probably remember it better than if you looked at it in near-darkness, because the trace is stronger.

Like old newspapers, photographs, and other methods for storing information, memories fade. As time goes by, it becomes harder to find a particular memory trace because it is "hidden" amidst everything else stuffed in your memory.

That's why it's necessary to *refresh* memories to make sure you retain them. If you had wanted to memorize the phone number of the local pizza parlor for a few years instead of a few seconds, it would be necessary to repeat it regularly over time. If the memory trace is frequently refreshed, it becomes strong enough to be absorbed into long-term memory.

2. *Attributes.* Mental manipulations make the information you're trying to remember richer. For example, you can improve your ability to remember the name of a person you just met by analyzing the nationality of the name, or by determining the number of vowels and consonants. Most people don't pay much attention to attributes like this, but doing so will definitely help you register the information in your memory.

3. *Associations.* Mental manipulations can also help establish associations between two or more items you're trying to learn. If you wanted to remember Bob Lincoln's name, you might associate it with Abraham Lincoln, Lincoln, Nebraska, or even the Lincoln Tunnel to help you remember it—or perhaps all three. As the number of associations between an item and other items in your memory increase, the memory trace becomes more meaningful. The more associations, the easier it is to retain the trace and retrieve from memory.

Patterns occur when an item has more than one association. Try singing the "Star Spangled Banner" from the word *gleaming* or reciting the "Pledge of Allegiance" from the word *stands*. Tough, isn't it? You probably know every word of both of these, but your associations form a line-to-line pattern starting from the first word.

***It's difficult to recite the Pledge of Allegiance from the word stands.** That's because of the pattern involved in learning it.*

---

4. *Retrieval tricks.* Finally, mental manipulations can provide a handy way to retrieve information that is otherwise buried in the corners of your mind. Many people
have learned to memorize the names of all the Great
Lakes by simply remembering the word *HOMES.* Each
letter is the first letter of the name of a lake (*H*uron,
*O*ntario, *M*ichigan, *E*rie, *S*uperior). Similarly, some people remember the colors of the spectrum by just thinking
of *ROY G. BIV* (*R*ed, *O*range, *Y*ellow, *G*reen, *B*lue, *I*ndigo,
*V*iolet).

On a more ordinary level, to remember that you
have to buy bread, eggs, Alka-Seltzer, and milk, just think
of the word *BEAM.* That one word, letter by letter, gives
you the whole list.

If you need to remember some information briefly
(like the phone number of the pizza parlor), strength manipulations are most appropriate. If you need to store it
more permanently, use the more powerful attribute, association, and retrieval manipulations.

The kind of memory manipulation you use depends on how long you need to retain the information.

Most of the mental manipulations in this chapter
will improve your ability to register information in more
than one way—usually in some combination of the four

categories. The more effects a manipulation produces, the better it works.

Learning Strategies

The following story contains many routine memory tasks which serve as examples of the mental manipulations to follow:

You went to a party and were introduced to several people. First you met Bill Frumpus (a chubby person) and after a couple of minutes, Sarah Smith (who has a medium build). You and Sarah discovered a common interest in golf, so you asked for her phone number. Later, George Abercrombie (distinguished-looking, with a gray beard and blue eyes) and Arlene Lorenz (also distinguished-looking), who were standing together, introduced themselves to you.

During the evening, you chatted with these people. Bill told you he was a mechanic and that he enjoyed pitching (especially curves) for a local baseball team. Arlene explained that she worked for a chemical firm, Alchemy Limited. George and Sarah work at a newspaper, the Des Moines Sentinel. *As you talked with these people, it became apparent that they were good friends with each other. They bowled together on a team and had even won a trophy.*

In the months that followed, you attended a conference with Bill and Arlene and took a history course with George and Arlene. Sarah helped you prepare a presentation you had to make at work. You read George's articles in the Des Moines Sentinel *concerning the nature of democracy and the kinds of government in Libya and Saudi Arabia. You got to-*

gether socially with the four of them. Your friendship grew to the extent that you even took turns at picking up groceries and doing chores for each other.

Let's take a close look at how each of the four basic strategies work to help you remember.

Strength Manipulations

There are two kinds of strength manipulations: those that foster *paying attention* and those that involve *rehearsal.*

Attention

These manipulations focus your attention on details that should be registered. They are important in situations where it's not enough to remember only the gist of information.

Mental snapshot. When attempting to remember a visual scene, scan it systematically, then close your eyes and question yourself about it; open your eyes and note what you missed. Repeat the cycle until you're satisfied that you've registered the scene in memory.

For example, to etch in memory the time your bowling team won a trophy, take a mental snapshot of the awards ceremony or a dramatic moment in the match.

To master total recall when it comes to details, there are three different manipulations you can use.

Sensual imagery. Imagine the information you're trying to remember with as many of your senses as possible.

For example, to remember the game of golf you played with Sarah, think of how the course looked, how you felt to be there, what the woods smelled like, the sounds you heard while playing, and the like.

Reflection. Reminisce about some event that took place in your life recently.

For example, when your head hits the pillow at night, try to reconstruct mentally an experience you had that day. Unfurl it in your mind, reflect on it, and see if it has some significance.

Rehearsal

Rehearsal is particularly useful when you want to keep a piece of information in consciousness, but don't feel it has to be in your long-term memory.

Acting out. Act out the information you want to remember.

For example, while studying for your history course with George and Arlene, let each person take the role of a historical figure and improvise dialog as you imagine how those people would talk.

Simple rehearsal. Repeat the items to be learned to yourself over and over in your head.

For example, on being introduced to Arlene, repeat to yourself, Arlene. . . Arlene. . . Arlene. . . Arlene. . . Arlene . . . Arlene.

Articulatory rehearsal. Repeat the items while carefully enunciating each syllable and noting the placement of the tongue in your mouth.

Repeating a word or phrase aloud and enunciating each syllable is one way to store information you need on a short-term basis.

For example, on being introduced to Arlene, repeat out loud "Ar-lene. . . Ar-lene. . . Arrrr-leeeene. . . Arrrrleeeene."

Cumulative rehearsal. Repeat the items in successively larger groups.

For example, when you leave the party, say to yourself, "Bill. . . Bill. . . Sarah. . . Bill. . . Sarah. . . George. . . Bill . . . Sarah. . . George. . . Arlene."

Rhythmic rehearsal. Repeat the items in a rhythmic pattern, either in syllables or with a certain beat that is pleasing to your ear. You may choose to insert the words into a familiar song.

For example, "I before E except after C" is a simple rhyme that we all use to remember how certain words are spelled.

Spaced rehearsal. Repeat the items to yourself at increasing intervals, with each successive interval being twice as long as the preceding one.

For example: after having been introduced to someone, say the name to yourself once, then wait one second and say it again. Then wait two seconds and say it again. Then wait four seconds, say it again, and so on. It has been shown repeatedly that this graduated system works better than concentrated studying.

Attribute Manipulations

People can be characterized as large or small, rich or poor, bright or dull. Objects can be described as heavy or light, rounded or angular, expensive or cheap. Ideas can be analyzed as interesting or uninteresting, simple or complex, positive or negative.

Anything that can be registered in memory can be characterized by a set of *attributes*.

The more attributes you include when you register a memory, the better. Each additional attribute you record about an event increases the strength of the trace, deepens your comprehension of detail, and provides another way to retrieve the information later.

Anything that can be registered in memory can be characterized by a set of attributes. Pay attention to your feelings about what you're learning.

These manipulations are designed to enhance your ability to register attributes. They're useful for learning information that is initially difficult or uninteresting and information that must be remembered in particular detail.

Feelings. Pay attention to your feelings about what you're learning.

For example, when you first meet George or Sarah, take pains to note anything you find particularly pleasing or repugnant about them.

Judgments. Make a judgment concerning the material you are trying to memorize.

For example, when you meet Sarah Smith and George Abercrombie, think to yourself that the name *Abercrombie* sounds more affluent than *Smith.* You may also make a mental note that George is a snappy dresser—or a terrible one, for that matter.

Description. Verbally describe to yourself what you plan to learn, and study your description.

For example, to make sure that you'll remember someone's face, describe the shape of the eyes, nose, and mouth to yourself. Notice that George has a dimple on his chin.

Meaning analysis (semantic). Think in terms of a dictionary definition of the information you're attempting to learn.

For example, when Bill tells you he is a mechanic, don't just file it away in your head. Analyze the meaning of the word *mechanic* (one who repairs mechanisms, usually automotive but also other machines). This may also serve to prompt you to find out more—what kind of a mechanic is Bill?

Phonetic analysis. Take note of the sounds that make up the information you are trying to remember.

For example, when Bill tells you that he is a mechanic, sound out the syllables of the word: *mech-an-ic.*

Priority ratings. Rate the relative importance of various memory tasks you have to perform.

For example, remembering the time of your airline flight is probably more important than returning your neighbor's cake tin. By making these ratings in your head, you will attend to all of your memory tasks more efficiently.

Question. Probe for more information about what you're learning.

For example, if you want to be able to remember what Bill and Arlene tell you about their jobs, pepper them with questions. Ask about who, what, where, when, why, under what conditions, how, how much, how many, and how often things happen.

The process of asking and receiving answers builds up durable memory. A side benefit is that most people will appreciate your interest in them.

Relating. Judge how an item to be learned might relate to you as a person or to something in your past.

For example, when Sarah and George tell you about their jobs at the newspaper, think about how the newspaper relates to you. Do you like the look of it? Do you feel it gives fair and balanced coverage of the news? This reflection makes it "your" newspaper and should help you relate to what Sarah and George tell you.

If you judge how an item to be learned might relate to you or something in your past, it will help you remember better.

Time intervals. Take note of the relative time intervals between things to be learned.

For example, when you meet all of these people at the party, notice that it was two minutes between meeting Bill and Sarah, and ten minutes after you met Sarah that you were introduced to Arlene.

Understanding. Look at the information you're trying to learn from several perspectives.

For example, if you are preparing for a presentation at school or work, put yourself in the shoes of various members of your audience—your teacher, your boss, the board of directors. Imagine that you are a different person reading your presentation.

Visual analysis. When information is presented to you visually, try to record in your memory what it looks like.

For example, when Bill says he is a mechanic, visualize the shape of the word printed out (*M*—two upside-down *V*'s joined; *e*—a pattern similar to Pac-Man; *c*—an *o* with a bite out of it; and so forth).

Association Manipulations

Things are easier to remember when they are learned in *association* with one another rather than alone.

Association manipulations enable you to relate different memory traces to each other.

Forged connections. When you need to remember two or more different things, try to determine if they can be connected in some way. Then rehearse both the items and the associations between them.

For example, suppose you had to buy some items at the store. In trying to remember milk, steak, soap, and shampoo, you may recall that soap and shampoo are associated as cleaning products, and so are milk and steak associated, since both involve cows.

Present with past events. Try to find a similarity between something you're experiencing now and a past event.

For example, when reading a story or watching a movie, think of how it is similar to or different from others you have experienced.

Relations (meaningful). Look for synonyms, contrasts, or other meaningful relations between two items you have to learn.

For example, you read in the paper that a certain country is in a state of anarchy. Think of another word that means *anarchy* (for example, *chaos*), or think of its opposite.

Relations (phonetic). Look for ways in which two or more items sound similar to each other.

For example, when you read a news story about the country of Libya, notice that *Libya* sounds like *tibia* (a bone in the leg) and *liberty.*

If you need to remember two or more different things, find some way to connect them. Or look for ways in which items sound similar to each other.

Relations (visual). Think of ways in which two words you want to learn are visually similar, or visually different.

For example, *Libya* looks a bit like the word *Arabia*, but very different from the word *Afghanistan*.

You can also see if the item to be learned looks like something that you already know. *Libya*, for instance, looks like the woman's name *Libby*.

Organization

Research shows that information that is *organized* can be learned four times faster than the same information presented randomly.

Research shows that organized information can be learned four times faster than information that is presented randomly.

Organization manipulations are useful when you have to learn a large number of items and the information conforms to a specific structure. For instance, it's easier to learn the periodic table of the elements than it is to learn each element independently.

Clustering (meaningful). When you have to memorize a list of things, try to group items that share similar meanings.

For example, when you meet Bill, George, Sarah, and Arlene, mentally split the group into males and females.

Clustering (phonetic). Match the items that have a similar sound.

For example, note that Sarah, George, and Arlene all have an *r* sound in their name, while Bill does not.

Diagram. Draw a picture on paper, showing any relationship between items to be learned.

For example, diagram that Bill and Sarah are friends. Arlene and George are friends.

Sequence. Arrange the items you need to learn in the order they were presented, or in an order you feel is most natural.

For example, think to yourself that the first person you met was Bill. Then you met Sarah, followed by George. The last person you met was Arlene.

Spatial arrangement. Notice how the things you have to learn are positioned in space.

For example, when you were introduced to Bill, he was leaning against the railing in the front hall. Sarah was sitting near the pool. George and Arlene were in the kitchen.

Alternate Records

For important information that you need to remember perfectly or nearly perfectly, alternate records are most useful. There are four types of schemes: *elaboration, reduction, transformation,* and *technical.* The easiest ones to learn and use are elaboration and reduction manipulations. Transformations are more difficult, and technical manipulations require the most effort.

Elaborations

Anyone who ever took a music course learned that "Every good boy does fine" is a handy way to memorize that the lines of the staff on sheet music are E-G-B-D-F. This is a mental manipulation in which you elaborate, or add something, to the information you're trying to learn to make it more meaningful.

To remember the names of the planets in our solar system, you could memorize "Meek violet extraterrestrials make just such unusual new pets (Mercury, Venus, Earth, Mars, Jupiter, Saturn, Uranus, Neptune, and Pluto)."

If you wanted to, you could think of "Never eat shredded wheat" to help you memorize the points of a compass. But in this case, it's like using a bazooka to swat flies. I've never met anyone who had difficulty remembering North, East, South, West.

Acrostic. Form a phrase in which the first letter of each word makes up the word you're trying to learn.

For example, to remember Bill's name, think of him as a "*b*rave *i*ntrepid *l*ovable *l*ug," or a "*b*umbling *i*diotic *l*umbering *l*out."

Limerick. Cast information to be learned in the form of a limerick.

Putting words into limericks or songs can help you remember them forever.

For example, "There once was the greatest of all bowling teams, made up of Bill, Sarah, George, and Arlene."

The familiar "Thirty days hath September. . ." is a rhyme that very elegantly makes complicated data almost second nature.

If you feel comfortable using this technique, you might like to check out two books that describe many other memory-enhancing limericks: *A Dictionary of Acronyms and Abbreviations* and *A Glossary of Acronyms, Abbreviations and Symbols.*

Image (color). Imagine the item you're trying to learn in one color against a different colored background.

For example, to remember the name of a product sold by Bill and Arlene's company, imagine it in bright purple against a violet background (if you prefer harmonious colors) or purple against bright green (if you prefer clashing colors).

The same process could be used to register a person's face. Use colors that catch your attention.

Image (symbolic color). Imagine the item you're trying to learn in a color that is symbolic of how you feel about it.

For example, upon being introduced to a new person that you like, register his or her facial features in silver or gold. If this person irritates you, paint the face red. If you dislike the person, use paint with a muddy color.

Image (graphic). Form a mental image of a word's letters as they are spoken to you.

For example, when someone tells you he will meet you on Tuesday, imagine the word *Tuesday* printed out.

When you make a date to meet on Tuesday, imagine the word Tuesday *printed out.*

Image (meaningful change). Change a word that doesn't stand out on its own into a more meaningful visual image.

For example, to remember that the newspaper Sarah and George work for is the *Sentinel*, imagine a one-cent coin being mailed to someone named Nell *(cent-to-nel)*.

Bridge. When you have to learn two items, think of something else that has something in common with both items.

For example, to memorize that Bill plays baseball and likes to throw a curve, you might register the word *round.* A baseball is a round object, and a curve ball travels in a rounded path on its way to the plate.

Number elaboration. When you need to memorize a series of numbers, think of them in terms of dollars and cents.

For example, suppose Sarah's phone number is 730-1957. Imagine that the two of you went out for dinner. Her entree might be $7.30 and the total tab might come to $19.57.

You may wish to change a meaningless series of numbers into seconds, minutes, years, or dates. Sarah's phone number might also be cast as July 30, 1957, or 7/30/57.

You can memorize a meaningless series of numbers quickly if you can associate them with something meaningful in your life.

Principle stating. Describe to yourself the meaning, significance, or theme of the material you are learning.

For example, after attending a play, state to yourself whether the play is a tragedy or a comedy. When people are asked to state the theme of something after they learn it, they remember it better.

Ridicule. Turn the information to be learned into a ridiculous name or pun.

For example, when Sarah tells you her last name is Smith, think of Sarah Smithsonian Institution, Sarah Smith Brothers, or some other combination that strikes you as funny.

Sentence generation. Create a sentence that contains the information to be learned.

For example, you could say, "I just met Sarah Smith, who lives in west Des Moines."

The sentence that you use doesn't necessarily have to be factual, but a true sentence has the advantage of supplementing the information you need to learn with other useful information. If you create a false sentence, make it blatantly so ("I just met Sarah Smith, who lives on Mars"). Otherwise, over time, you may be inclined to remember the sentence as fact.

Story generation. Create a short story that contains the items to be learned.

Create a short story that contains all the items you need to learn.

For example, you might say, "Once upon a time, Bill lived in the city. To make his living, he worked as a mechanic. . . ."

Reductions

While elaborations add to the information you're trying to learn so it becomes more memorable, reductions take away. You may prefer them to elaborations because they are shorter. Reductions, in fact, work very much like shorthand.

Abbreviation. Form a smaller word by using a few letters from a large word.

You can remember a large word by forming a smaller word using a few of the same letters.

For example, runners and other athletes who wear polypropylene clothing refer to it as polypro.

Bleaching. Imagine the item to be learned in black and white.

For example, think of Arlene's face as a black and white photograph.

First letter coding. Take the first letters of a list of words and make them into a different word.

For example, think of George, Arlene, and Bill as *GAB.*

This is a form of an acrostic. You can also add extra letters to the basic skeleton to make another word, such as *GARBLE.*

Sentence reduction. Form a word or words out of the first letters of some of the words in a sentence.

For example, "We the people of the United States" can become "White pot, U.S."

Summary stating. Identify key words in a passage that stand for the overall theme.

For example, the Pledge of Allegiance can be encoded as: "one nation," "conceived in liberty," "all men created equal."

Transformations

These manipulations change the information you wish to learn to make it different in form but related in a meaningful way.

Synonym. Think of the closest synonym to the word you're trying to learn.

For example, when you want to remember that a certain country is a democracy, think to yourself that it is also a "free state."

Antonyms and synonyms are useful for memorizing words.

Contrast. Think of the closest antonym to the word you're trying to learn.

For example, when you want to remember that a certain country is a democracy, think to yourself that it is not a "totalitarian state."

Class member. Think of words that are in the same class as the word you need to learn.

For example, to remember that a country is a democracy, note that its citizens enjoy the same freedoms as those of Canada, Great Britain, and the United States.

Sound-alikes. Think of one or more words that sound like the word to be learned.

For example, suppose you read that some other country is a dictatorship. Think of that as "dictate or ship."

Technical Schemes

These manipulations are called *technical* because they require more involved instructions and depend on a system you memorize ahead of time. They're also sometimes referred to as mnemonics. Technical manipulations have been around for hundreds (and sometimes thousands) of years, and they are the strategies most often equated with memory improvement.

A warning about technical schemes: You'll need to put in a great deal of effort to use them well. Nevertheless, if you're willing to make the effort required to use these methods, they are highly effective for memorizing material. If you feel comfortable with technical schemes, by all means use them. You may also want to read a few books that concentrate on them exclusively: *How to Develop an Exceptional Memory* and *Improving Your Memory Skills.*

Link. When you have to learn a list of things, form a mental image that connects the first and second items, then an image connecting the second and third items, and so on.

For example, to learn the bowling team's names, form an image of Bill handing a bowling ball to Sarah, Sarah throwing the ball, George setting up the pins and giving the scoresheet to Arlene.

Loci. To learn the same list of things, imagine a familiar building and mentally place each item in a different room.

To learn a list of things, mentally place each item in a different room of your house. Then pass through the house and gather them up as you attempt to remember them.

For example, for the bowling team, mentally place Bill in the foyer, Sarah in the living room, George in the kitchen, and Arlene in the dining room.

It's helpful to have several loci locations in mind: your office building, church, golf course, and so on.

Number/letter conversion. Translate numbers into letters using this code:

> *1 = t, d, or th*
> *2 = n*
> *3 = m*
> *4 = r*
> *5 = l*
> *6 = g, j, ch, or sh*
> *7 = c, k, hard g, or q*
> *8 = f, ph, or v*
> *9 = p or b*
> *0 = z, s, or soft c*
> *Vowels are not assigned a number.*

For example, to remember that Columbus discovered America in 1492, code the number *1* as *t*, *4* as *r*, *9* as *b*, and *2* as *n*. This converts 1492 to *TRBN*. Since TRBN is meaningless, a couple of vowels can be added to make the word *turban*. Now, if you need the year of Columbus's discovery, think of a turban. You can reconvert the letters and "remember" the date.

Developing your own code for remembering things can be a useful tool when you don't want others to know what you're doing.

This scheme can also be used to register words. The name *Bill*, for instance, is coded as 955 (*b* = *9*, *l* = *5*, and the *i* is ignored because it is a vowel).

Peg (alphabet). Assign the following words to the first four letters of the alphabet: *a* = *ace*, *b* = *bee*, *c* = *sea*, and *d* = *deed*. Mentally "peg" words you're trying to learn to these words.

For example, imagine Bill holding an ace, Sarah being pursued by a bee, George standing in the sea, and Arlene performing a good deed.

Peg (image). Memorize the following rhyme: "One is a bun, two is a shoe, three is a tree, and four is a door." When you have to learn a list of things, associate each item with a peg word by mentally constructing an image that contains both of them.

For example, suppose you had four chores to do: go to the library, grocery store, gas station, and meet George. Imagine the library coming out of a bun, a shoe in the window of the grocery store, a gas station up in a tree, and a picture of George plastered over a door.

Another way to use pegs is to choose peg words whose first letter visually resembles the number. For instance: *1 = ice, 2 = zoo, 3 = beer,* and *4 = ant.*

You may also experiment with the "rotten peg" system, using displeasing or offensive peg words: *1 = limburger cheese, 2 = dog feces, and 3 = sour milk.*

As you've probably guessed, you could invent an alternate peg system around any topic that interests you (such as food, movies, or rock stars).

Peg (verbal). This time, the pegs are *1 = smart, 2 = cunning, and 3 = exciting.*

For example, to register chores to be done at the library, grocery store, and gas station, you might form the following sentences: "The library is for the smart." "The grocer advertises specials in a cunning manner." "It was exciting when the gas station blew up."

Forgetting and Retention

"Will you remember me tomorrow?"
"Oh, yes!"
"Will you remember me next month?"
"Of course!"
"Will you remember me in a year?"
"Surely!"
"Will you remember me forever?"
"Undoubtedly!"
"Knock, knock."
"Who's there?"
"See! You forgot me already!"

In a way, memories are like old newspapers. You can save them, but as the months and years go by, they begin to fade. They get covered up by other old newspapers and become harder to find. The information becomes less relevant as time goes by. Sometimes you accidently throw them away and they're gone forever.

Why We Forget

In some cases, a memory trace disappears for physiological reasons. Alcohol, as we know, kills brain cells (and with them, the memories they contain). So do high body temperatures that come with illness.

In other cases, the memory trace doesn't disappear, but it is altered. You may intentionally "revise" an original memory to trumpet a personal triumph or to protect yourself from the pain of a traumatic event.

Like a tape recorder, your memory system seems to record new experiences over old ones, causing the old

---

Your mind will unintentionally revise an original memory to protect you from an unpleasant thought.

---

memories to be "erased." It's doubtful that the brain erases just like a tape recorder, but there is considerable evidence that we "unlearn" past information and skills.

Suppression is an example of a situation in which a memory trace is completely intact, but you can't retrieve it. This is a normal process necessary for survival in an information-loaded world. For example, when you're starting up a new project, it's natural and healthy to put your last project out of your mind. Some degree of repression is also normal, but extreme cases may be a sign of adjustment difficulties.

Finally, there are situations where just part of a memory trace disappears. When this happens, memory becomes error-prone. You've probably had the experience of seeing a person you recognize but can't name, or of recognizing one person as someone else (mistaken identity).

To further complicate matters, different kinds of memory tasks have different rates of forgetting. Skilled actions are frequently remembered indefinitely. It's said that nobody ever forgets how to ride a bicycle, and I have yet to come across anyone who has. Events and intentions, on the other hand, are generally not retained nearly as well.

Pseudo-forgetting

Very often what seems like a case of forgetting is simply a case of never having learned a piece of information in the first place. Perhaps you didn't pay attention when the information was presented, or you didn't realize you were supposed to remember it, or you didn't understand it. It's also common for a person to "forget" some information or past experience because of impaired eyesight or hearing that prevented its full registration in his or her memory system.

So we forget things because the memory trace fades away, is altered, suppressed, repressed, erased, or is never fully registered in the first place. Or it could be a combination of these factors. For this reason, the best way to improve your memory is to learn a wide variety of mental manipulations that will help you register, retain, and remember effectively.

Retention Manipulations

There are only a few mental manipulations that focus exclusively on *retention*. Each affects one or more of the different causes of forgetting.

These manipulations require some degree of discipline. But when the task is sufficiently important and you don't have confidence in your ability to remember, one or more of the following will prove well worth the effort:

Review periodically. Use this manipulation if you fear that the information won't "stick" because it's uninteresting or foreign to you. Every time you reexperience the same piece of information, your memory of it is strengthened. If you need to commit something to memory, review it repeatedly until you reach the level of accuracy you're aiming for. At this point, an occasional glance should prevent a memory loss due to decay, distortion, interference, suppression, and unlearning.

When you do your review, try to use the same mental manipulations you used when learning the material the first time.

Avoid similar information. Sometimes the information you're learning may become confused in your mind with other material you are studying or have already learned. If possible, avoid having to learn two types of similar material at the same time. People who try to learn two foreign languages simultaneously often find the words of one interfere with learning the words of the other.

Never study two similar subjects at one time, and make sure you get plenty of rest and sleep while in the learning process. Interference from outside sources will diminish your ability to retain what you're learning.

Sleep or rest. Another way to avoid confusion when you are learning something new is to sleep as much as possible during the learning period. When you sleep, the memory system doesn't have to encounter new information that might interfere with or suppress what you already learned. Of course, this only makes sense if the learning period is brief.

Anticipate remembering situations. This manipulation is helpful if you worry that you might not be able to retrieve the information you need when you need it. Imagine situations in which you might be called on to remember something. This will help you recognize the cues that were present when you were learning and stimulate the memory to emerge when it is needed.

Make moderately unpleasant memories meaning-ful. Perhaps you forget things because you find the topics unpleasant to think about. If you have to write a thank-you note to somebody you don't like, for instance, take steps that will lead you to avoid suppressing the memory. Think of reasons why it's crucial that you remember. Consider the consequences if you forget. Imagine how good you'll feel when it's all over.

What Did He Know and When Did He Know It?

Sometimes, you might prefer to suffer a memory loss. Spies, organized crime figures, and some politicians often wish they didn't know or could forget certain infor-mation. But occasionally, all of us have a bad day we'd like to forget.

Mental manipulations for intentional forgetting haven't received much scientific attention. Other than tak-ing your mind off the unwanted memory by distraction or change of scene and time, there isn't much you can do. But the purpose of this book is to enhance memory, not to diminish it.

Retrieval Strategies

You can use mental manipulations not only to learn information and retain it, but also to *retrieve* information buried deep inside your memory. Of course, as in archae-ology or gold prospecting, there's no guarantee that you'll dig up what you're searching for. But by using retrieval manipulations, you are likely to come up with more infor-mation than if you had made no effort at all. And the more manipulations you try, the better your chance for success.

Successfully storing a thought in your long-term memory is one thing, but the ability to retrieve it on a moment's notice requires another type of mental manipulation.

Retrieval manipulations bring a memory trace from long-term memory into consciousness by stimulating the surrounding traces or part of the trace itself.

Frequently, if you can dig up a part of a memory, you can recover the whole thing. This situation comes up all the time: You remember when an event took place but not where, you recognize a person but can't place a name, you recall your opinion on an issue but don't remember the reasons, and so on. If you focus your attention on the part of the memory trace you know, it is possible to activate the desired trace, causing it—with a little luck—to emerge into full consciousness.

Even if you're not quite that lucky, you may be able to reconstruct the memory and make an educated guess. For example, you may think to yourself, Okay, I know I met that guy in 1987. Let's see. . . I spent that summer in Chicago, so it could have been at that convention. . . he had to have been with ABC Corporation. . . now I remember! His name was Herb Dunn!

Try these manipulations to help make an educated guess at the memory item you want:

Alphabet search. Ask yourself which letter of the alphabet began the name, word, or thing you're trying to recall. For example: "A? Alan, Al, Alvin, Andrew. . . B? Bill, Bob, Robert! His name was Robert!"

Free association. Recall everything you can that is associated with the information you're trying to remember. Then try to recognize any actual attributes of the memory trace among the associations you generated.

For example, in trying to remember directions to a place you visited previously, think of the names of streets, stores, or landmarks on the way, and then see if you recognize any of them as being on the route you're trying to recall.

Question. Ask as many relevant questions as you can about the information you're trying to retrieve: Who? What? When? Where? Why? How? How much? How many? How long? How often?

This is particularly useful when you're trying to remember the nature of a complicated event. People can rarely remember all of the necessary details without a multiquestion approach.

If you can remember part of a memory, you should be able to retrieve the whole thing by doing a quick mind search. There are ten methods of searching from which you can choose.

Reinstate mood. Think of the mood you experienced when the memory was registered. Try to recapture it.

Tip of the tongue. Guess the length, number of syllables, infrequently used letters, doubled letters, or other unusual features of the word to be remembered.

The manipulations below help dig up a memory trace by associating it with other information. They're most useful when you recall very little or none of the trace.

Causation. Recall the circumstances in your life that might have prompted the memory you wish to remember.

Surroundings. Imagine the surroundings you experienced when the memory was registered. Ask yourself what you were doing, saying, or thinking at the time.

Retrace. Try to remember what happened just before or right after the event you wish to remember.

Return to the scene. Mentally go to the place where you first learned the material. Try to spot features of the room or site that connect with the memory itself.

Recall manipulations. Try to think of any mental manipulations you may have used when you learned the material.

Use 'Em or Lose 'Em

Some of the mental manipulations in this chapter may seem obvious, but the truth is that many people fail to use them when memory situations come up in everyday life. Here's a suggestion: Copy the manipulations you find particularly useful on an index card and keep it in your wallet or purse. The next time you're stumped, pull the card out and run through the manipulations.

The strategies discussed in this chapter are sure to boost memory performance in many situations. That boost, however, has a price tag—time and effort. If you have time

---

The only way to make a mental manipulation work for you is through practice and patience.

---

to execute the manipulation and if the memory task deserves the effort, these mental manipulations can be the best way to deal with your memory stumbling blocks.

Summary

Different kinds of mental manipulations work for different people and for different memory tasks. Manipulations strengthen memory traces, relate them to other memories, organize them, or work them in some way to make them more meaningful.

Forgetting is caused by decay of the memory trace, as well as distortion, revision, unlearning, inattention, suppression, repression, and interference. Retention manipulations work to solve these problems through review, making unpleasant memories meaningful, avoiding the interference of new memories, and anticipating memory situations.

Retrieval manipulations make a memory trace emerge into consciousness by stimulating the surrounding traces or part of the trace itself.

Mental manipulations require a lot of practice and discipline if they are to work effectively. Comb the wide range of manipulations and choose the ones that suit you best.

Chapter 7

MEMORY SUPPORT SYSTEMS

After reading through dozens of mental manipulations in the last chapter, you may be asking yourself, Why do I need all of these memory tricks and strategies to remember things? Why not just write everything down? Then I'll never forget anything.

That's true. The only problem is that if you made a note of everything that happened to you so you would remember it later, you would spend all of your time jotting down notes instead of experiencing life. The human memory is an efficient machine that usually doesn't need to be replaced by pencils and paper.

However, life in the information age is jam-packed and hectic. You can supplement your memory to tremendous advantage by using external memory aids. When you set an alarm to remind you to take the clothes out of the dryer, you're using an external memory aid. When you make a list of items to be picked up at the supermarket, you're using an external memory aid. You're also using an external memory aid when you put letters to be mailed next to the front door as a reminder to take them with you the next time you leave the house.

Modern technology has come up with a lot of gadgets and tools to help us with memory. Take advantage of them.

There are hundreds of these aids that can relieve you of having to perform memory tasks in your head. They have been used for centuries. In some ancient African tribes, people used a "memory stick," carving important symbols of events into the stick so they would be remembered later.

For certain people and certain situations, memory aids work wonders. Surveys taken with both young adults and the elderly show that people use memory aids to cope with remembering more than they use mental manipulations. In fact, even memory experts admit that they use external aids more than mental manipulations.

Are Memory Aids a Crutch?

A few memory experts insist that we should not use external memory aids. In their view, such aids reduce your reliance on your own memory, and this weakens your overall ability to remember.

In some ways, that makes sense. Since the invention of the pocket calculator in the 1970s, there's not much need to perform mathematical functions anymore, and math ability for some people has suffered. Wouldn't a "memory calculator" have the same effect—taking the place of your real memory and damaging your powers of remembering?

It's true that using an external aid for a memory task—especially over a prolonged period—can cause that skill to wither slightly through disuse. As an example, suppose you buy a telephone that stores the numbers of your friends and "speed dials" them at the push of one button. Using that phone may reduce your ability to memorize phone numbers.

However, your ability for other tasks will not lessen. Using a telephone with computer memory won't affect your ability to remember the rules of games or past events of your life.

Memory aids may lessen your ability at certain repetitive memory tasks slightly, but they more than make up for that by allowing you to devote your attention to more important things. By using a notebook to remind you of appointments instead of using your memory, you'll never miss an appointment, and you can direct your thoughts toward the content of your appointments instead of when and where they will take place.

Using external memory aids, such as automatic timers and to-do lists, can help take the hassle out of your life and keep your mind clear for more important tasks.

A long time ago, Plato argued that the masses should not be taught to read. He believed that if the knowledge of the world were available in books, people would no longer strive to acquire it. Well, reading has done pretty well over the years, and the more people read, the more they seem to thirst for knowledge.

Similarly, the more you remember, using whatever means are available, the more you'll want to remember. The way I look at it, let's use all the help we can get.

How to Choose and Use Memory Aids

Your choice of an external aid should be based on how well it applies to the memory tasks that interest you. Frequently, a memory aid that promises to be effective turns out to be useless. For example, a piece of string tied around a finger is almost universally recognized as a reminder. But in fact, this aid has limited value because it doesn't tell you *what* you're supposed to remember.

Another example of an ineffective memory aid is the recently developed electronic key chain that is supposed to help you find your keys by beeping when you whistle or clap your hands. Unfortunately, the key chain beeps in response to just about any sound, so it's more of an annoyance than a memory aid. Someday, perhaps, the device will be improved so it can really help people with this common memory problem.

Some people write information they want to remember on their hands. This might work for you, but do you really want to have ink all over your hands? Many people appreciate state-of-the-art commercial aids, like memory watches, but others feel they require too much time and effort to use. Your choice of external memory aids should rest on a realistic appraisal of whether they suit your tastes.

New Study Buddies

Anyone who ever took an exam in school realizes the value of taking notes. The very act of writing notes helps your recall later. Putting information down on paper forces you to organize the information you're trying to learn and focus your attention on the key points.

Taking notes has been shown to improve memory retention. It's one of the oldest memory aids around.

Besides taking notes, there are several other memory aids that can facilitate studying.

Teaching Machines

Machines that teach have been around for decades, but the technology of the 1990s offers a wealth of options. In addition to the latest Sylvester Stallone movie, your local video store offers tapes that will help you learn about virtually any subject imaginable in an hour or so. Computer stores stock shelf after shelf of software that makes it possible to learn interactively, a technique that has been shown to accelerate learning.

High-tech teaching tools such as videos and computers can be highly effective.

These high-tech teaching machines have certain advantages over teachers and formal classes: They're less expensive, they're available to you at any hour of the night or day, and they allow you to learn at your own pace, in privacy.

Memory Art

Not many people use art to aid memory anymore, but it was very common in times long ago. In the fourteenth, fifteenth, and sixteenth centuries, artists painted floor plans of houses, cathedrals, amphitheaters, and other locations so people could mentally place information in different areas to memorize it. This is called the *method of loci.*

You can do the same thing today. If you have an interest in Europe, you might hang a map of the continent on your wall. When you have a list of items to remember, mentally "place" each item in a different country. Repeat the placements to yourself several times now and then. When you need to recall the list, mentally "take a trip around Europe," picking up the items as you go.

You can use a map to remember a list.

Memory by Superstition

Have you ever known somebody who would make sure to wear a "lucky hat" or carry a "lucky pen" when he or she had to take an examination? People sometimes use a certain object in the semi-serious belief that it will enhance memory.

These superstitions are particularly common among college students, but it's not unusual to find businesspeople who have a special suit, briefcase, or tie that they save for really important memory situations. It's all pretty silly, but if you did especially well while wearing a particular piece of clothing in the past and it makes you feel confident, I say, go for it. It won't hurt you any, and it may help by putting you in a mental state conducive to remembering.

When you have to put your memory to a test, a good luck object can give you confidence.

Information at Hand

A good chunk of mankind's knowledge can be placed on a few bookshelves a fingertip away from your desk at work or home. To back up your memory, keep external knowledge sources handy: notes, professional books, catalogs, instruction manuals, atlases. Every office should have a good dictionary and thesaurus. Popular reference books like *The Guinness Book of World Records*, *The Farmer's Almanac*, and an encyclopedia are useful. Several companies make electronic dictionaries: When you type in a word on the keypad, the correct spelling, pronunciation, synonyms, and definitions jump to the screen in seconds.

Build a reference library that will help you get smarter.

All of these sources keep facts on hand so you don't have to bother remembering them. Of course, they also provide you with information you never knew. The human brain has been likened to a file cabinet. But along with a brain, it's always helpful to have a well-stocked and well-organized file cabinet around.

Business meetings and school lectures are often easily forgotten. It helps to take careful notes and review them later. But if you find it difficult to keep up with a fast-talking or confusing speaker, it may be better to get the whole speech on tape. At relatively little cost, you can pick up a microcassette recorder that is no larger than a pack of cigarettes. The disadvantage of taping is that every minute you record is a minute that you'll have to listen to later, so you may want to limit your recording to important situations.

If you come across a passage in a book or magazine that you may need to know about later, there's another new electronic miracle that may help—the portable photocopy machine. It actually fits in one hand and can make a good quality copy on a strip of paper the size of a cash register receipt.

The "Memory-Friendly" Desk

When you're working, you don't want to waste time or break your concentration to hunt around the office for a folder, contract, or office gizmo. You won't have to if your desk is "memory-friendly." Keep the top of your desk in an order that facilitates finding what you need. Items that you use every day—pens, stapler, scissors, tape, and the like—

should be on top of the desk and handy. Things that you use occasionally should be in a convenient drawer that is organized with compartments. If you only use something on rare occasions, don't clutter up your life with it. Put it in a closet or other storage area.

An organized workspace will keep clutter out of your mind.

You don't have to be neat as a pin, but your system should be consistent and organized. Office supply stores sell all kinds of desk organizers and specialized devices that hold eyeglasses, business cards, or rubber stamps. All of these things are geared toward organization. The more organized your life, the less likely that you will spend time rooting around for items you can't find.

Unforgettable Obligations and Appointments

Whether you live in New York City or on a farm in Kansas, you need to be aware of schedules, appointments, and events in your life. The best way to deal with these memory burdens is to use a record system that will manage details for you.

For many people the primary record system is an appointment book, and there are many kinds available. Other people keep a to-do list on paper, erasable board, or computer. The key is to make a note of your appointment, obligation, or chore the instant you first think of it. When you hang up the phone, immediately jot down any commitments you made. If you wait until later, you're relying on memory, and that defeats the very purpose of using an external memory aid. The act of keeping a daily record of planned activities forces you to review the events of the day and insures full awareness of your obligations.

Appointment books and to-do lists are essential.

Of course, the most organized appointment book in the world is useless if you don't keep it handy. Choose one that is compact enough to carry with you wherever you go. This way, you can always record a thought or make note of a date and closely monitor what needs to be done.

It's a good idea to keep memo pads in key places around the house or office: in the kitchen, upstairs, and certainly in the car. Some people put a pad at their bedside in case a thought occurs to them in the middle of the night. You can even buy a pen that has a built-in light so you can write in the dark without disturbing anyone.

Some people record each obligation in several separate places. This provides added mental rehearsal of the details of these obligations. But it can be tricky because you might record an obligation in one place and not in all of them.

Keep a calendar in one or more rooms of your home or office. Some people prefer to have their calendar out of view, so they use a pocket calendar or appointment book.

Others must have a visible, prominent calendar like the popular day-at-a-glance calendars that hang on the wall and have plenty of room for notes. Of course, you can buy a watch that displays the date, or affix a tiny metal calendar to your watchband.

Timing Is Everything

The note you wrote about that important meeting isn't going to jump off the page, grab you by the lapels, and send you on your way. But there are devices that virtually do that for you. The standard clock radio, for example, is so commonplace that we don't even think of it as a memory aid. Most include a "snooze button" that lets you lie in bed for a few more minutes but doesn't let you forget to get up. These days you can buy models that have two alarms, so two people who need to wake up at different times can do so without resetting.

A smart person knows the importance of being on time, every time.

Once you're out of bed, you'll keep track of the time with your watch, some of which beep to remind you of appointments or even give you a little message on a display screen. Some watches that store information can be attached to a personal computer to transfer phone numbers, flight schedules, and other information back and forth.

At the office, you can use a computer program that sets off alarms and displays messages at predetermined

times, even when you're using the computer for other purposes.

It's not necessary to spend a lot of money for a
machine to beep, buzz, or light up and remind you when
it's time to do something. A plain old mechanical windup
kitchen timer that sells for a few dollars can also be used
to let you know when your favorite TV show is coming on,
when to wake your spouse from a nap, or when it's time
to make that important phone call.

Symbolic Reminding Techniques

When you're in a hurry and don't have time to make
a note or set an alarm, you can improvise an external
memory aid very simply by making an obvious change in
your physical environment. For example, the phone rings
just as you're rushing out of the office for a meeting. It's a
business associate, who asks you to drop by later in the
day. You don't have time to make a note, so you turn your
wastebasket on its side and place it in the middle of your
office. When you return after your meeting, you just about
trip over the basket, which instantly reminds you to stop
in and see your associate.

This system, called *symbolic reminding*, increases
the likelihood that you'll remember because seeing the
object in such an unusual place symbolizes a memory task
yet to be done. The negative aspect of this technique is that
the change you make may remind you to do *something*,
but it doesn't tell you *what* that thing is. Still, symbolic

Try These Suggestions for Symbolic Reminding

- Pick up a small object and carry it until you've accomplished your memory chore.
- Put a paper clip in a buttonhole or the pocket of your shirt.
- Connect a cord from your wrist to your belt (moderate or large gestures will simultaneously pull on your wrist and belt).
- Put a knot in your handkerchief.
- Position your furniture in an odd way.
- Put a rubber band around one wrist.
- Put a piece of tape on one finger.
- Put your wallet in a different pocket.
- Put your purse over the other shoulder.
- Switch your watch from the usual wrist to the other wrist.
- Switch your wedding ring to your other hand (make sure you tell your spouse).
- Turn your watch face down.
- Wear your belt tighter.
- Wear "memory" jewelry, such as a special bracelet, necklace, or tie tack that you reserve for this purpose. Choose jewelry that's hard to forget—unusually heavy, noisy, or glittery.
- Wear your clothes in an unusual manner. If you normally wear a certain article of clothing—like a vest or a sweater—don't wear it. Or wear something you normally wouldn't wear, like an ascot or a scarf. To be most effective, memory clothing should be unusual in design, pattern, or color. If you're feeling especially bold, put on a loud tie or a shocking scarf to remind you that something has to be done today. Outrageous polka dots always attract attention. And every time somebody comments on your attire, it's a natural reminder of why you're wearing that article of clothing.

reminding does the job for many people, and it is among the most popular memory aids.

Symbolic reminders can really work in a pinch.

If symbolic reminders don't do the trick, make your reminders *explicit*. Stick a reminder to yourself in a spot where you can't help but see it: on the front door, a frequently-used mirror, your computer screen, the steering wheel of your car, the lid to the toilet. Post-it Notes are convenient and easy to use.

Another option is to put up a message board. It will provide a constant reminder of things you have to do.

Your "Take-Away" Spot

We have all had the experience of being out the door and on the road when we suddenly realize we left something important behind. To avoid this, reserve one place in your office or home where you routinely put things that need to be taken away. During the day, when you come across something that has to travel with you, put it in that spot. Then, as you get ready to leave, you know that everything you need to take with you is in one easy-to-check place.

Designate one spot in your house and at the office to put things you might forget to take with you.

To be most effective, your take-away spot should be convenient and near a major exit. A table near the front door is ideal. Get into the habit of checking it every time you walk out the door.

A particular coat pocket or a section in your purse or wallet can be designated as a portable take-away spot for certain things you must have with you. Plane tickets, theater tickets, checks, and important papers are some of the easy-to-lose items that could be put there. Having a single portable checkpoint will save you the time and worry of searching through all of your clothing to find an important item.

Touch-Tone Recall

If you dial a particular phone number very frequently, you'll eventually memorize it even if you're not trying. For the rest of the calls you make, storing the numbers in a little black book, Rolodex, or business card file is a lot easier than bothering to learn them all by heart.

The disadvantage of *any* paper system is that people inevitably move, get new phone numbers, and, sometimes, new names. In a few years, your phone directory is a mess of scribbled and confusing changes. Enter the microchip. Many companies make electronic pocket organizers that are essentially little black books on a chip. When information is stored *electronically,* it can be easily sorted, updated, or erased so your list of phone numbers is always organized. Many of the new telephones store 10 to 100 numbers in their memory so you don't have to store them in *your* memory.

You can also purchase a portable telephone dialer that stores your frequently-called numbers. When you hold the device against the telephone handset, it generates the tones that dial the number. Your personal computer can also dial the number for you if it is hooked up to a phone line with a modem. And if you should leave the house or office and forget to turn on your answering machine, it is possible to activate the machine with a call from outside.

Take advantage of the electronic age and get a load off your mind.

If you have trouble remembering what was said during your important telephone conversations, you may want to consider recording them. Just about every telephone manufacturer makes a model that uses the tape from its built-in answering machine to record conversations at the touch of a button. Any electronics store will sell you the inexpensive cables needed to hook up a standard cassette recorder to your telephone. If you do record your conversations, etiquette and the law require that you inform the other party.

Minimize Travel Traumas

Long-distance travel can be a pain in the memory. Not only are you in totally unfamiliar surroundings, but you're required to perform tasks that you don't do every day—dealing with luggage, language differences, foreign currency, and so on. Memory failures are frequent, but if you prepare in advance, they can be minimized.

Frequent flyers should keep a checklist for packing posted in their luggage.

It's no fun to arrive at your destination and realize you forgot something you need. One system for avoiding this is to make a list of all your regular travel necessities and keep it in your suitcase. Then, when it's time to pack, take out the list and gather the items that you know you need. You can also buy a travel kit that contains the usual toiletries. If you *do* forget something, hotels will happily (for a fee) provide toothbrushes, shampoo, razors, and other commonplace products you may need during your stay.

Time, Money, Language

If there's anything that confuses travelers, it's figuring time and currency in a foreign location. If you travel often, you may want to consider purchasing a travel clock that shows what time it is in each of the world's 24 time zones. You can even buy a hand-held calculator that lets you punch in the exchange rate for the local currency and instantly does the conversion for you.

As a traveler you tend to use credit cards frequently, and you don't want to forget your card at a cash register when you're thousands of miles from home. To ensure against this, you can buy an electronic credit card case that sets off a beep alarm if you close it without putting back your card. Don't leave home without it.

You can also buy a pocket translator that will help you with the language of the country you'll be visiting. You

Currency exchange computers, travel clocks, and pocket translators can do a lot of your thinking for you.

just type a word into a keypad and the translation appears on the screen. Of course, if you prefer a lower-tech solution to the language barrier, there are dozens of foreign language phrase books that can also serve as your memory aids. All of these products are sold in department stores and specialty shops for travelers.

When working away from the office, you may need general office materials such as note pads, folders, a stapler, forms, or certain tools. One way to eliminate the inconvenience that results from forgetting these items is to prepare a "portable office." By keeping a fully stocked package, you'll have only one take-away to remember as you rush to the airport.

Another memory task that comes with a vacation or a business trip is keeping track of your luggage. To make sure that you recognize your bags (and someone doesn't mistake yours for hers), mark them so they'll be conspicuous. Besides the usual luggage tags, attach a bright ribbon, yarn, or personalized strap to the handle. The same goes for cameras, musical instruments, and other objects you carry separately. Your passport should be readily at hand and well protected, too. Some people keep theirs in a zippered pouch around their neck or waist at all times so they'll never forget it.

Travel is usually one of the more memorable experiences you have in your life, but you inevitably forget details of a trip as months and years go by. Documenting trips as you go safeguards an accurate recollection of them. In addition to pasting photos in an album, save your ticket stubs, maps, itinerary, and other mementos you pick up along the way. Shoot videos. Keep a travel diary. Label your photos carefully because sometime in the future you may want to go back and recall the name of that hotel or restaurant or that unusual man you met. With a permanent record of the trip, you can refresh your memory and make it seem as though it were only yesterday.

Keep Your Personal History Handy

You don't have to limit yourself to vacations to keep records of your experiences. The act of keeping a daily record or diary facilitates memory in three ways. First, it relieves memory of having to retain all the details of an event. It also fosters a better memory of the event because the process of making a record provides a review of what happened. Finally, the notes will enhance your recall later.

Mementos of all kinds serve more than sentimental purposes. They provide the clues necessary for you to remain close to the positive aspects of your past. Some people complain that these things just create a lot of clutter, but clutter to one person may be the key to memory for another. That rock you picked up at the family campsite may be the

---

A collection of travel souvenirs will keep happy memories fresh for a lifetime.

---

trigger for a flood of memories that bring back the wonderful time you had when you were there.

You won't always have photos or mementos of a time you wish to remember. On these occasions, try to find sensory cues that might help an old memory to emerge. Playing music on records or tapes that you associate with the time period is a powerful memory aid.

The sense of smell is also a way to return to the past instantly. The aroma of pine needles reminds people of holiday time. Burning wood reminds us of summer campfires. A distinctive perfume and the smell of a certain food can also provide a potent cue to moments otherwise lost to time. Some products are specifically intended to link experiences and past memories with fragrances. A few years ago, a company was marketing "fragrance records" that gave off specific smells intended to awaken old memories.

Art may also suggest a past period or event. You might hang maps or paintings of places you want to remember or posters of old movies, rock groups, or political campaigns.

Finesse with Finances

Like going to the dentist, paying bills is one of those painful life experiences we often prefer to forget. If you're disciplined, you can combine all your bill-paying obligations by setting aside a few hours each month to do the dirty deed. It may help to choose a naturally memorable date, such as the first, fifteenth, or last day of the month. You don't have to rely on your memory to keep bill-paying day in mind. Just write "BILLS" on that date in your calendar or appointment book for every month of the year.

To make sure that you don't misplace bills waiting to be paid, gather or label them in some conspicuous fashion. As soon as you pay a bill, put a mark on it. When bills arrive in the mail, put them all in your bill folder and keep the folder in one place so you can find it easily when bill-paying day arrives.

Another problem that many people have is balancing their checking account. With automatic teller cards and credit cards so popular these days, it's more difficult to determine exactly how much money is in your account. You can't be expected to remember all your transactions and the amounts of each.

Many companies make inexpensive checkbook calculators that make the job of tracking accounts easier. Basically, they are calculators that let you punch in your deposits and expenditures and store a running balance for your checking and credit card accounts. Some computerized devices even remind you when to pay your bills or complete other financial obligations. Don't be concerned if you, like many people, are more comfortable with plain old pencil and paper for doing these jobs.

One nice thing about living in the computer age—even for people who don't use computers—is that many businesses and financial institutions do a lot of tiresome chores for you. Some employers will direct-deposit your paycheck in the bank of your choice, so you don't have to bother. Similarly, your bank may pay certain bills for you by simply deducting the money from your checking account (with your permission) and automatically sending a check

---

Take advantage of all the conveniences that make handling home finances care-free.

---

to the other party, so you don't have to remember to do it. The government's Payroll Savings Plan provides for a deduction from your paycheck to buy U.S. Savings Bonds, to help you build up your savings. The plan is even advertised with the slogan, "Do you forget to remember to save?"

Any of these systems will reduce your financial memory load considerably. There's no need to suffer the embarrassment and hassle of forgetting to pay a bill, deposit checks, or put money away for the future.

Memory Aids for Staying Healthy

When you were a kid, Mom and Dad remembered anything you were supposed to do to take care of your health. As an adult, you're on your own. You have to remember to eat right, exercise, see doctors as needed, and take medication when appropriate. Plus, you have to remember all of these things for your own children. Now there are many aids that help you take care of yourself.

Cooking

The microwave oven, of all things, is actually a nifty memory aid. Because it can thaw out frozen food so quickly, you don't have to remember to take food out of the freezer hours ahead of time. That means you can prepare a nutritious meal on short notice, and you don't have to fall back on fast foods because of a memory lapse.

You can purchase egg makers that automatically stop cooking when the eggs are done and kettles that turn themselves off when the water level in them gets too low. The age-old whistling teapot is a kitchen memory aid, as is the hourglass timer and the recipe file.

Certain devices can make you a genius in the kitchen.

All of these devices can help you manage cooking a meal, which sometimes seems like conducting an orchestra. When putting together a complicated dish, you may find it helpful to set out all of the ingredients you'll need in advance and line them up on the counter in the order they will be used.

It's also a good idea to label leftovers and frozen foods with the date of storage, so you can be sure to use the older items first and thus avoid spoilage.

Dieting

When you diet, you have to remember what foods you ate, when, and how much. And for most dieters, these are memory tasks they never had to bother with before.

There's no memory aid that will prevent you from overeating, but there are several that can help you keep track of your diet. You can keep a pencil and paper record of every food you eat, of course, but that can be time-consuming and tedious. People who go on the Weight Watchers program receive a printed checklist that makes it much easier to record the types of foods and how many portions of each are eaten every day. For a more detailed record, you can purchase several calculator-type devices that will tell you the amount of sodium, carbohydrates, protein, fat, and other nutritional attributes of just about any food. Some of these are also available as software you can run on your personal computer. Some stand-alone devices have a built-in scale and will tell you the nutritional components of a portion of a particular food based on its weight.

Speaking of weight, scales are getting more and more versatile. You can now buy a high-tech scale that will not only tell you how much you weigh today, but also how your weight has fluctuated over the last six months. It's getting harder to forget how you're doing with your diet.

Exercise

We all lead hectic lives. Between work and kids, plus taking care of everything that needs to be done with the house, we often forget to exercise. The best way to make sure this important task gets done is to *schedule* it as though it were a meeting, appointment, or some other obligation. Write it into your appointment book and calendar. Don't think of it as something you'll do if you have any extra time at the end of the day—treat it as a serious commitment. If you arrange to exercise with another person, you automatically add memory aid for the task—and an extra incentive to keep at it.

Taking Medication

There are two kinds of memory aids that will help you remember to take your medication: passive devices and active devices.

Did you or didn't you take your medication? A buzzing pillbox will make sure you never have to guess again.

The most common are *passive* devices that remind you when you happen to look at them. A good example of a passive device is a pillbox that has several little compartments. If you divide up the pills you need to take during the day or week and place them in the appropriate slots, it's easy to see how many you took, and when—provided that you remember to look at the pillbox at all.

If you tend to skip your medication times entirely, you need an *active* device. Pharmacies and stores that specialize in medical supplies sell pillboxes that signal you with a light, a beep, or a buzzer when it's time to take your medication. A watch with memory settings can also serve this purpose. You can even get computerized pill-bottle caps that record when they were opened or closed, so you and your doctor can check on how well you have been following instructions.

Keeping Track of What's Yours

One of the most familiar—and probably the most annoying—memory problems is losing things. If we all had a nickel for every minute we've spent hunting around the house for our keys or wallet, we'd all be rich. Putting objects down somewhere is such a mundane act that we are frequently unaware while we're doing it. No wonder we can't recall the experience.

The simplest way to prevent this problem is to be organized. By that, I don't mean you should be obsessively neat and tidy. The fundamental principle is to put your various possessions in the same place all the time. By sectioning off your drawers, cabinet shelves, closets, and shoe boxes and putting things in their place, you always know where they are. The organizational scheme does the remembering for you. Inexpensive toolboxes, tackle boxes, and sewing boxes help to make organizing small objects easy.

Always forgetting where you've put something is aggravating to you and others. Yet it's a problem that's so easy to solve.

Labeling

Sectioning off all of your possessions into hundreds of little compartments won't help much if you can't quickly identify what is in each one. But if you put labels on all of these containers, you can tell at a glance what is in any one of them, and you can quickly find the things you're looking for.

If you tend to misplace things, think about getting personalized items. It's not expensive to buy pens, pencils, lunch boxes, camera straps, and other objects with your name and address printed on them. Labels should also be put inside articles of clothing, especially for children and others who tend to leave items of clothing behind when they visit friends or go to public places. Several years ago I visited a museum in Styal, England, where I came across a book titled *Where Is It?* Some family in the mid-nineteenth century used it as a memory aid. The book listed dozens of valuable possessions and a description of where each was located. You can do the same thing today with a plain notebook. Carefully list all of your valuable possessions, including when and where you bought each one and how much you paid for it. Then be sure to store the book in a convenient place for ready access.

A record of this sort is important, especially when it comes to home insurance. When people are asked to recall what they own, they generally forget many items because of the sheer number of their possessions. However, the insurance company will cover only what you *know* you own. If someone were to break into your house or apartment and steal thousands of dollars worth of your things, could you remember the items without a *Where Is It?* book?

One good way to get around losing things is simply to make them harder to lose. If a neighbor keeps borrowing your tools and forgets to return them, tie a colorful piece of yarn to each of the tools or paint them a bright color. It will remind him that they're not his and identify them as yours when you see them. The reason hotels often add a large attachment to each room key is because guests commonly forget they have the key and accidentally walk off with it. However, when there's a piece of leather as long as your forearm attached to the key, you are more likely to remember to drop it off at the front desk when you check out. Use a similar trick for keeping track of keys and other small items at your house.

Don't set your possessions up for mistaken ownership.

If you tend to misplace your own keys, you'll never do it again if you have a special place for them. A hook near the door or a little bowl on your dresser should serve the purpose nicely. If you prefer to keep your keys on your person at all times, you can buy devices that fasten keys to your belt, bracelet, or other parts of your clothing.

Just in case, make a duplicate set of your keys and put it in a special place or give it to a trusted neighbor. You can also purchase a small metal box that holds several car keys and attaches to the underside of your car—no more lockouts in lonely parking lots far from home.

Appliances That Remind *You*

Remembering to turn your household appliances on and off at the proper times not only saves money in energy bills, but prevents fires and other accidents as well. These days, manufacturers put microchips into just about every type of appliance, and this can ease your memory burden substantially. We are all familiar with VCR's that turn on and off to record TV shows when we're not home. You can also get inexpensive devices that click lights on and off at preset times. There are irons that turn themselves off automatically when you leave them lying flat on the ironing board for longer than 30 seconds. Outdoor sprinkler systems can be programmed to turn on and off automatically. A gadget you can stick in the soil of a houseplant makes a sound if the soil dries out, reminding you that it's time to water.

The list goes on and on. The next time you buy an appliance, check for any special memory functions it might have. Why not search for the product that not only does the job, but facilitates memory too?

Buy appliances with memory functions.

Shoppers' Helpers

The standard shopping list on a little piece of scrap paper is a memory aid that serves its purpose perfectly for many people. You know exactly what items you need and can go to them directly instead of relying on your memory or wasting time cruising up and down the aisles.

Another alternative is a preprinted list. Checklists remind you of items you might forget otherwise. They are quicker to fill out than a written list and spare you the effort of trying to remember what you need to do or buy. You can buy checklists like these or make one of your own and photocopy it.

Don't get caught short in the kitchen. Learn how to keep a foolproof grocery list.

Post a grocery checklist prominently in your kitchen. Attach a pen or pencil on a string nearby. When you notice that you're running low on something, put a check mark next to that item on the page. When you go grocery shopping, just take the page with you and you have a fully filled-out shopping list.

You can also save yourself the trouble of remembering to buy some things by buying in bulk. Obviously, you can't buy a year's supply of milk all at once. But some products such as toilet tissue, toothpaste, and canned goods that you use all the time can be purchased in large quantities. Not only will this ease your weekly shopping burden, it will also save you money.

Checklists and to-do lists are indispensable memory tools.

Getting "caught short" at the checkout counter can be embarrassing. Many grocery stores sell a simple hand-held tally counter that adds to your total with every click of a button. These also come in handy for jobs that require counting things: inventory, money, the number of people who walk through a turnstile. When the numbers get into the hundreds, a momentary distraction can disrupt your concentration and force you to start all over again. With a machine to do the "remembering," you can turn your attention to more important things. Baseball umpires use a variation of this device, and they only have to remember three strikes and four balls!

Coupons

You can save a lot of money on food bills by using coupons, but not if you leave them home when you go shopping. If this happens to you, keep your coupons in your wallet, purse, or the glove compartment of your car. It is also a good idea to keep a coupon file that is divided into different categories. Every few months, go through the file to get rid of coupons that have expired. The more organized your coupons are, the more likely you are to use them.

Parties

Throwing a party requires you to perform many extra memory tasks: remembering who should be invited, remembering to send the invitations, keeping track of all the food, drink, and special gifts. Party suppliers can provide individual systems that help you keep track of table settings, guest lists, and menus.

To keep track of what your guests are drinking, do what professional bartenders do. Serve your drinks in dif-

The shape of a glass can be the clue to what it contains.

ferent-shaped glasses. If Frank orders a brandy, the distinctive shape of the traditional brandy snifter will serve as a reminder if he asks you for a refill.

Diversions

Even having fun requires using your memory. If you intend to play a game well, you need to know the rules and be able to recall them quickly. Most games have certain general procedures that increase the players' chances of success. Bookstores stock crossword puzzle dictionaries, anagram dictionaries and spellers, books on Scrabble, chess, Monopoly, and even Pac-Man. For general parlor games, pick up a copy of *Hoyle's Book of Rules*. And wait until you get a look at the devices available for pursuing various hobbies. For example, you can buy hand-held calculator-type devices that keep track of golf scores, help you keep up with your horoscope, and remind you of odds for betting the horses.

Why argue over the rules? Keep the official rule book handy.

New Ways to Remember Special Days

"We are dedicated to those millions among us who—for one reason or another—forget birthdays, anniversaries and other special occasions. Our members relax—while we do the remembering for them!" So goes an advertisement for "The Reminders Club," a Massachusetts service whose sole purpose is to remind people of upcoming special occasions in their personal lives.

It's just about impossible to forget Christmas and New Year's, but your Aunt Rhoda's birthday might slip your mind. If you don't send her a card or give her a call, she may be hurt and upset. There are several ways to prevent such problems. When you buy a new calendar for next year, write in your special days and dates right away so you won't have to worry about remembering them. Some people buy a year's worth of birthday cards at the beginning of the year, address them all in advance, and send them out as the days come up. Stationery stores and card shops sell all kinds of systems for reminding yourself of special days.

For more active reminding, you may want to invest in a pocket organizer with an alarm function. If you can program one to beep when it's time for your important meeting, you can program it just as easily to beep on the morning of Aunt Rhoda's birthday.

A small investment in a pocket computer will prevent you from ever forgetting your anniversary again.

Sources for Memory Aids

You can find the memory aids discussed in this chapter in stationery, department, and electronics stores. You may also want to check mail-order catalogs, especially those that specialize in high-tech devices. A few to look in are: The Sharper Image, P.O. Box 26823, San Francisco, CA 94126-6823; Markline, Dept. W, 14 Jewel Dr., Wilmington, MA 01887-9988; Sporting Edge, 22121 Crystal Creek Blvd., Bothell, WA 98021; and Exeters, 6 Hughes, Suite 100, Irvine, CA 92718-1901.

Summary

External aids can be extremely helpful in relieving you of memory tasks so you can concentrate on more essential things in your life.

Learning and remembering may be facilitated if you use: appointment books, memo pads, calendars, checklists, notes, knowledge sources, teaching machines, memory art, superstitious objects, timing devices, symbolic reminders, labeling, a consistent take-away spot, smart appliances, various hand-held calculator devices, and, perhaps more than anything else, solid organization.

Chapter 8

HOW TO REMEMBER THE 100 THINGS YOU'RE MOST LIKELY TO FORGET

In the past few chapters, you discovered many social, mental, and external strategies for learning, remembering, and retrieving information. Each of these techniques could be used in a variety of situations. When you mentally repeated the phone number of the pizza parlor, for instance, you could have used that technique just as easily to memorize someone's name, directions to a place, or the formula for the circumference of a circle. It's a general mental manipulation.

But if you want to respond better to any particular memory situation, it's best to learn a technique that is designed specifically to deal with that task. Being *prepared* to handle a specific kind of memory situation is half the battle of remembering.

Blasting out of Your Memory Sand Trap

Let's say you play golf. Every once in a while you'll find yourself caught in a sand trap. You might choose to wait until your ball lands in that sand trap to figure a way to blast out of it. Or you might consult a golf pro about the specific technique for getting out of sand traps and practice before your next round. If you do the latter, you'll be less rattled, you'll have the tools you need, and you'll probably handle the situation better when it comes up.

Memory has its sand traps, too. To blast out of them, you want to use what are called *task-specific manipulations*. These memory strategies are geared toward just one or perhaps two memory tasks. Task-specific manipulations are not as versatile as general mental manipulations, but they're usually more efficient and more effective. They serve to prepare you for solving specific memory situations that are troublesome.

For many memory situations, there is only one best way to come out the winner.

Consider the common problem of remembering to water your plants. You could jot down a note to yourself and stick it up on a bulletin board. Or you could use one of those "plant alarms" that set off a tone when the soil doesn't have enough moisture in it. The note on the bulletin board is a general reminder. The plant alarm is only used for that one particular situation. Chances are, the plant alarm will be more effective in alerting you to water the plants than the note will.

Bartenders tend to have an excellent memory for drink recipes. Waiters and waitresses are often remarkable at remembering which customers have ordered what. Professors are, well, *fairly* good at remembering books and articles in their field. These personal memory skills we acquire through practice are *specific*. That bartender who can memorize recipes for drinks so easily is probably no better than the average professor or waitress when it comes to remembering appointments. Even the greatest memory experts in history had a *specific* memory talent. Not one of them was known for having a great memory overall.

Bartenders aren't geniuses because they know how to make every single drink in the book from memory. They've simply mastered the task-specific manipulation.

Use this chapter as you might use a dictionary. Look up memory situations that plague you, then look at strategies that address those situations. Here's an example of a specific memory task, and a technique to prepare for it.

Combination to a lock

Registration: Visualize the numbers in their positions. Mentally rehearse opening the lock. Associate the numbers with ages of your life and a significant event of each of these ages. Notice mathematical properties of the numbers (what they are divisible by, and how the numbers relate to each other mathematically, such as one being about twice the other). Write the combination down and save it. Write it in an inconspicuous spot near the lock.

A visualization method will prevent you from forgetting the combination to a lock.

Remembering: Recall the mathematical association you formed. Try to recall the feel of turning the tumbler. Consult notes.

The memory task is to remember the numbers needed to open a combination lock. Several techniques are provided to help with the problem. Choose the one that feels most comfortable. Use it whenever you can and practice it in your head, even when a combination lock isn't handy.

Keep a record for two to four weeks, indicating how often you tried the combination, whether you used the technique, and how successful it was. Decide if it works for you. If it doesn't, try to figure out why. Is it because you're not yet skilled at doing it, or are you simply unsuited to the manipulation? If the latter is your problem, pick another manipulation that might work better for you. Follow the same process for each of the tasks in the chapter.

If you think you're forgetful, you are not alone. Most people are plagued by the same silly little problems.

Following are specific mental manipulations for 100 everyday memory situations. I chose these because they were rated "important" by my students in memory improvement at Hamilton College, Clinton, New York, and by people who participated in my research at the Center for Aging and Cognitive Research at the University of Manchester in England. The entries are divided into the four types of memory situations: knowledge, events, intentions, and actions. For all entries, there are suggestions for both registering information and for remembering it.

Knowledge

Answers you know but can't recall

Registration: To avoid being caught in this situation, review your knowledge of the topics that are likely to come up when you meet with a particular group. Be armed with information others expect you to know.

Remembering: Use the tip-of-the-tongue formula— try to think of the number of letters, odd combinations of letters, the number of syllables that make up the word you want to recall. Make notes about related ideas to see if they trigger the answer. Reflect on key terms. Ask the speaker to paraphrase the question. It will often trigger— or even contain—the answer. Stall; the answer may come if you give it time.

Names of authors

Registration: When you read the material, associate your reactions to it with the author's name. Note to yourself what other works have been written by the author. Analyze the name for unusual characteristics (such as rare letter combinations or ethnic origins). Keep a notebook of works you've read that are of special interest to you. Discuss literature with people you know.

Knowing the proper way to register something in your mind is the key to remembering it when you need to.

Remembering: Try to recall when and where you read this work. Try to remember if you discussed it with anybody. (See also "Names of old acquaintances" on page 201.)

Information on an unfamiliar topic raised in conversation

Registration: Study up on possible topics of discussion prior to a get-together. Keep abreast of events. Consult newspapers, magazines, encyclopedias. Ask an informed friend to prime you on the unfamiliar topic.

Remembering: It's easy to come across as naive or foolish in this situation. Don't jump into the conversation right away. Let the conversation elicit what you *do* know. Admit your short supply of knowledge on the subject. If you don't recall *anything*, remain quiet.

Current events

Registration: As you read or listen to the news, note a half-dozen key events. Test your recall of these events. Read newspapers and news magazines regularly.

Discuss events with your mate or other friends often. Associate current news with previous events.

Remembering: Reflect on your key events. Skim through a news magazine. Ask others for their impressions of a certain event or of current events in general. Their responses may trigger your own thoughts.

There are mind tricks for remembering dates, places, and historical events.

Important dates in time

Registration: Keep a notebook of dates you want to remember. Use it to refresh your memory before scheduled events in which remembering dates will be useful.

Remembering: Try to recall how you learned the date. Think back to any associations you might have formed when you first learned it.

Geographical locations and terrain

Registration: In your mind, visualize the outline of the geographical area. Compare the shape to something you know. (Italy looks like a boot.) Verbally describe the shape to yourself. ("Texas has a V shape on the bottom, left and right sides, and a flat and rectangular protrusion on the top.") Make sketches of the area in relation to other areas near it and see how close you come. Refresh your memory occasionally by looking at a map.

Remembering: Recall how you learned about the geography. Scan a globe or atlas when you have the time and opportunity.

Grammatical usage

Registration: Don't try to *memorize* grammar rules, try to understand the logic behind them. Test your ability to articulate the grammatical problems present in poorly formed sentences. (Most grammar books include such drills.) If you notice that you're forgetting what you learned, test yourself and restudy.

Remembering proper grammar isn't a matter of memorization. It's a matter of using logic.

Remembering: Recall how you learned the grammatical point in question. Think about its logic. Consult a grammar book or someone who knows grammar well.

Historical facts

Registration: State the fact, paraphrase it, and think about how it came about and what resulted from it. Imagine the event in your mind. Relate past facts to current events. Keep a notebook of important historical facts and review it periodically. Read books on the historical era that interests you and highlight parts of the text that you consider important. Find someone with similar historical interests and have discussions. Make flash cards.

Remembering: In your mind, reconstruct the time period. Conjure up associated images. Consult your notebooks. Initiate conversations on historical subjects.

Information you've read

Registration: Analyze the author's purpose. Is it an expression of fact or opinion, analysis of a problem, or an advancement of a new idea? Write down important points in the form of an outline. Mentally summarize each paragraph or section after reading it. Take notes. Read in a quiet place, without distractions. Glance at notes occasionally. When you reread the material, try to predict what the author will say.

Analyze authors as well as their books and you'll never forget who wrote what.

Remembering: Imagine the place where you did the reading. Mentally reconstruct the material. Check your notes. Mull over the surprising or unusual facts you've learned.

Jokes and anecdotes

Registration: Identify key words in the joke and link them in succession. Imagine the figures and the event depicted. Keep a notebook of favorite jokes. Buy joke books. Review your notes or books before a situation where jokes might be told.

Remembering: Don't start telling a joke if you're unsure of the ending. Run the joke through in your mind before you tell it. Consult your notes surreptitiously if you need a refresher.

Foreign languages

Registration: Use simple rehearsal: Repeat vocabulary words. Review rules of grammar. Associate or link unfamiliar English words to words or roots of the foreign language. Practice reading and speaking (silently and aloud). Use what you are learning as often as possible. Listen to tapes—spoken word and musical—in the language. Watch foreign language television and try to read publications in the language. Seek out people who speak the language fluently and engage them in practice conversation. Try to visit the country where the language is spoken.

You can learn a language more effectively out of the classroom.

Remembering: Think of English words that share a root or might be similar to the foreign language words in some way. Think back to your classes, your teacher, and textbooks. Consult two-way dictionaries and grammar books.

Foreign phrases for travel

Registration: Make a few flash cards for yourself— foreign word or phrase on one side, English on the other.

Stick to essential words or phrases such as "Please," "Thank you," "Where is the bathroom?" And do no more than half a dozen at a time. (If you try to do too many, you are likely to give up.) Ask a native to check your pronunciation; the process of doing so will also help you to learn. Use the *interactive imagery* technique: Form an image of the object that a foreign word reminds you of, and associate the image with the English word. For example, *caballo* (pronounced *cab-eye-yo*) is the Spanish word for *horse*. To learn this word, form an image of a cab with an eye on its side and the cab driver yelling "Yo" to a horse.

Remembering: Guess at the word's length and its first letter. If this does not help, try to recall the situation in which a native taught you to pronounce the word or a time when you did recall the word successfully.

Content of lectures and meetings

Registration: Try to predict what the speaker is going to say next. Pay special attention to statements that summarize points and phrases that emphasize important points. Take just enough notes to remind yourself later, but not so many that you are too busy writing to learn anything from the lecture. Review your notes periodically.

Making a game out of a boring lecture will improve your attention span.

Remembering: Try to recall the summary statements and most important points. Use these as a launch pad to bring back other points. Imagine the situation as it was when you first learned the material.

Lyrics of songs

Registration: Try to determine the message of the lyrics, not just the words. Note words that rhyme, then the phrases that lead to them. Learn phrases one at a time. Sing the lyrics, and note the rhythm of the music to associate it with the lyrics. Look at the sheet music. Listen to recordings and review them repeatedly.

Remembering: Recall the message of the song. Think of which sounds were the basis of rhyming and reconstruct which words contained those sounds. (Also see "Poetry" on page 180.)

Systems for solving math problems

Registration: Practice many similar problems. Solve them forward and backward. Use flash cards. Explain to someone else how the problem is solved. Substitute real life examples for the numbers. Practice, practice, practice.

Even if you're bad at math you can learn it more easily than you thought.

Remembering: Think of problems you have solved that are similar to the one you are trying to solve. Review problems you were unable to solve without this system and demonstrate how easy the solution is now.

Tunes

Registration: Sing or play each phrase and attempt to recall it from memory (either vocally or on an instrument). Repeat successive phrases and notes which have similar or recurring structures. Imagine the notes on sheet music. Associate the music with the lyrics. If there are no lyrics, make some up. Study the sheet music. Review and practice.

Sing along and you'll never forget the words again.

Remembering: Recall the structure of the song, especially recurring or distinctive phrases. Tie the tune to its composer and similar-sounding songs by him. Repeat the phrase that includes the comma, plus any other phrase you can muster.

Phone numbers, other numbers

Registration: Examine the number for any mathematical relationships (816 can be thought of as *8 and 8-times-2*). Translate the number into dollar amounts (*$8.16*), weights (*8 pounds, 16 ounces*), or historical dates of interest to you (*1816*). Translate the digits into corresponding letters on the push-button phone, then see if there is a word or phrase you can make out of the letters. Attend to the tones of the numbers while dialing. Record the number in a phone directory or memory dialing device.

Remembering: Try to recall how you learned the number (the math pattern or letter associations). Try to conjure up the "rhythm" of the number as you heard it or said it. Consult your directory, dialing device, or phone book.

Poetry

Registration: Learn line by line. Pick out key words. Note patterns of phrase structures that are similar or different across lines. Say the lines with emphasis. Characterize the poem's meter. Use rhythmic rehearsal— say the lines with a singsong or tonal variation. Get the beat of each line and associate it with the beat of the last line. Recite the poem to a friend and discuss its meaning.

Remembering: Recall the poem's theme. Think of any rhyming words. Recall the poem's structure and rhythm. Call up word sounds.

Prose

Registration: If you need to learn the gist of a passage, here are eight useful steps:

1. Reduce paragraphs to about six key terms.
2. Diagram the paragraph or draw a network of its ideas.
3. Note the signposts to content—the title, headings, topic sentences of paragraphs, illustrations, and summary.
4. Analyze the relationships between key terms, generate synonyms for the key terms, and associate them with a memory manipulation.
5. Read the passage aloud, emphasizing important points.
6. Picture the scene.
7. Paraphrase and simplify the passage.
8. Write a summary.

Learn the eight-step method of memorizing poetry the easy way.

In addition, you may wish to follow the SQ3R study formula (survey, question, read, recite, and review), which has long been used to assist focusing study efforts. However, recent research indicates that study formulas are usually not effective unless the formula prepares you for a certain kind of prose, such as scientific writing. (If you need to learn a passage verbatim, see "Poetry" on the opposite page.)

Remembering: Call to mind the paraphrases, analyses, and images you used in learning. Tell yourself the story or define the gist of the information in a few simple sentences: Boy meets girl; boy loses girl; boy finds girl. Then add as many details as you can. Talk about it with others.

Game rules

Registration: Buy a book on game rules. Review the rules before playing the game. Identify the conditions that lead to success and those that thwart winning. When you are surprised about a ruling, notice what just occurred and why. File it away in your head, or even on paper, for future reference.

Remembering: Think of the logic of the game and then reconstruct the rules. Refer to notes or rule books. Play the game at every opportunity.

Lines for a role in a play

Registration: Identify the attitude of superiority and inferiority of one character with other characters. Imagine yourself in the role with others. Note key terms, phrases, and postures associated with the role. Imagine performing the responsibilities and obligations that go with the role. Discuss with others how a good or bad role model might behave in the role.

Remembering: Recall the attitude that goes with the role. Think of people you know who have similar characteristics and "hear" them speaking the lines. Think of key terms and phrases. (If you need to learn only the gist, see "Speeches" below. If you need to learn the lines verbatim, see "Poetry" on page 180.)

Speeches

Registration: Identify key terms in the speech, and associate them in sequence using the method of loci. Go over the substance of the speech repeatedly. Rehearse as frequently as time allows. Consider what points will affect the audience most and concentrate on what leads up to each of these. Imagine the faces of your listeners as you make these revelations.

Public speakers don't have superior memories. They know the secret to "memorizing" the speech.

Remembering: Recall the key terms and ideas. Think of how they are linked. Be mindful of the message you want to leave with the audience. (Also see "Prose" on page 180.) Think of meeting the members of the audience after you give your speech and try to guess which parts of your speech they will want to discuss.

Spelling

Registration: Sound out words. Break long words into syllables. Note when the actual spelling differs from what experience would suggest. Write the correct spelling several times. Visualize it and make a mental note of it. Attend to potential trouble spots such as double letters or *ie.* Memorize rules of spelling given in spelling books and grammars. Practice by having people quiz you. Give quizzes to others.

Remembering: Recall spelling rules that might apply. Sound out the word, write it on paper, and judge whether that spelling "looks" right. Think of a similar sounding word you know how to spell. Use a computerized spelling checker.

Trivia

Registration: Imagine ways that questions might be phrased to test your knowledge of a fact. Test yourself to see if you can still recall facts you knew before. Catalog information of interest in a file or on a computer. Develop a "trivial" friendship, in which you and another quiz each other regularly and often. Bookstores and libraries have many titles aimed at preparing people for trivia games. If you develop a genuine interest in acquiring knowledge on many subjects, you will pick up a lot of trivia without trying.

Remembering: Try to remember where you might have learned and who might have taught you the facts desired. Did you learn the fact in a previous trivia game? Use the tip-of-the-tongue method: How long is the name? How many syllables? Study the reactions of others playing or observing the game. The faces of those who know or don't know may tip you off to the answer. Start to pronounce the first syllable of the answer you think is correct, and watch the reactions of people who are most likely to know the answer.

The tip-of-the-tongue formula can help you recall even the most trivial things.

Vocabulary

Registration: If you know something about the meaning of stems and roots of words, analyze how the word suggests its meaning. Attend to the syllables of the word. Try vocabulary quizzes in magazines. Play word games. Keep a dictionary on your desk. When you come across a word you don't know, look it up and make it into a flash card. Test yourself frequently with your flash cards. Form friendships with people who value words, especially crossword puzzle enthusiasts. Buy a new vocabulary book and check on what you know.

Remembering: Think of the length of the word, the first letter, and any related words. Browse through a dictionary under the suspected letter. Browse through a thesaurus under a related word.

Songwriters and singers

Registration: When you first hear a song you want to remember, associate your emotions and any images the song evokes. Read the album cover. Note to yourself what other songs resemble the new one, and in what way this song is unlike any other. Keep a notebook with the names of songs, their composers, and their performers. Form friendships with people who like to discuss music and music trivia. Play records and tapes of songs you like, then test yourself. Have others play records for you and try to identify the artist. When you find yourself listening to piped-in background music, try to identify it.

Stun your friends. Identify the composer as well as the singer of all your favorite songs.

Remembering: If you have a feeling that you know a song, try to recall when and where you heard it. Try to imagine other ways the song could be performed; perhaps that will give you a clue to when you first heard it.

Events

Personal routine duties

Registration: Foster an awareness of each action you perform: hanging up your coat, ironing the next day's shirt, brushing your teeth. If you are alone, describe your movements out loud as you do them. Routinely end the action in a certain way. (Leave your toothbrush pointed to the left after you brush in the morning and to the right after you brush at night, for example.)

Remembering: Think of possible consequences of the action, or what might happen if it's not done. Seek physical evidence that the action has occurred. To determine if you brushed your teeth, for instance, you might run a finger over your toothbrush to see if it is damp.

Birthdays

Registration: When you find out a person's birthdate, see if it is close to that of someone else you know. Try to cluster as many such dates as you can. Find an association between the person and the date. Steer conversations to birthdays or horoscopes and make mental notes. Keep records of birthdays in your calendar/diary, appointment book, or other commercial memory aid.

Remembering: Try to recall when this person last celebrated his or her birthday. Scan a calendar and try to narrow it down to a season or a month. Ask the person about his or her zodiac sign.

Cards already played in a game

Registration: Constantly review the cards that are played. Comment out loud as the cards are played, or mutter to yourself if your opponents complain. In a friendly game, it is usually allowed to ask, "Did you just play. . . ?" Play slowly to allow more time for encoding the cards. Try to guess which cards in a suit remain to be played. If you find it overwhelming to remember every card, prioritize certain cards to remember. Use a mental shorthand, such as *JHRTS* for *jack of hearts*. Take notes, if allowed.

A method of mental shorthand will help you improve your odds in a card game.

Remembering: Reconstruct what cards have been played according to the logic of who did what to whom in the game. Calculate rough odds by noting which cards are already face up on the table.

What you were saying when interrupted

Preparation: Before the conversation, anticipate what is to be discussed. This fosters better encoding. Evaluate the conversation: Is it interesting, trivial, seditious, salacious, and so on? Summarize the conversation to yourself. Resist being interrupted. Keep focused on the conversation and treat interruptions as peripheral.

Remembering: Sometimes it will come back if you just pause for a moment. If not, reconstruct the conversation and guess what was most likely said. Say something that might cue the other person to pick up the thread of the conversation. "You were saying?" will frequently cause the other person to summarize the conversation up to that point.

Details of past conversations

Registration: Reflect on each conversation as soon as it ends. Was it important enough for others to care about? Would the place where you had it and who was there be pertinent?

Remembering: Try to recall the situation, the location, who was involved, and what positions were taken.

Recall counter arguments. Think of the topic and attempt to reconstruct it. Look at paper notes if you have any.

Reconstruct past conversations accurately.

Dates of future events

Registration: Associate the date with the event. Associate one event with another on the same date. Associate the date with a past historic event that took place on the same date. A December 7 birthday is easy to remember because it falls on Pearl Harbor Day. Imagine a calendar with key dates marked. Record the event on your real calendar and in your appointment book. Scan your calendar every morning to see what events are coming up.

Remembering: Think of upcoming holidays or special days and see if you can recall any personal events you might have associated with them. Imagine your calendar or appointment book.

Verbal instructions for a procedure

Registration: Make sure you have the instructions right in the first place. Ask the person to repeat them, even if you think you registered them correctly. Going over them again gives you a second rehearsal. If there is another person with you, ask if he or she understood the instructions. The discussion will provide extra review and also establish an alternate source should you forget part or all of what was said. Reflect back on the instructions. Make notes.

Remembering: Imagine yourself in the situation where the instructions were given. Try to recall the first instruction in the sequence and reconstruct from there. Consult someone who was present when instructions were given, or find someone with experience or knowledge of the subject. Consult notes.

Directions for a travel route

Registration: When someone is giving you directions, ask for landmarks at each important choice point. When he or she is finished, ask your source to repeat the directions. Then repeat them to your source, to confirm them and give yourself another rehearsal. Try to remember the steps of the directions systematically: "First you. . . Next you. . ." and so on. Confirm the directions with a fellow passenger. Keep a notepad and pen in the car and use them to make a crude map or draw your route on a printed map.

Get in the habit of repeating things aloud.

Remembering: Reimagine the directions in map form. Try to reconstruct the logic of the recommended route. Consult with your map or a fellow passenger. If all else fails, stop and ask someone else. Your first source may have given you incorrect directions, or you may have misunderstood them.

Childhood events

Preparation: Save mementos and photos. Organize them in a scrap book. Reminisce with relatives and friends. Spend some of your solitary leisure time day-dreaming about highlights of your life.

Remembering: Think of landmark events in the same time period. Recall *boundary events*—such as the first day of school or graduation—that mark the beginning or the end of the period. Examine old toys and scrapbooks to elicit memories. Question relatives who were present at the time.

Events important to you

Registration: Decide ahead of time which things will be worth attending to and remembering. Anticipate the way the event will unfold. Describe the gist of the event to yourself right after it happens. Select a few key words that capture the event and rehearse them in your mind. Discuss the event with others right away. Make mental or physical notes about important aspects of the event.

Use your imagination to envision what will occur at a future event.

Remembering: Recall the theme of the event and try to reconstruct the event from there. Check for sensory details; real memories tend to have more sensory details than imagined ones. Recreate the scene in your mind. Recall major landmarks at the event. Imagine yourself at different spots in the location of the event, watching from different perspectives. Question yourself about particular attributes of the event; recalling one or two will often trigger others. Recall the event in a different order, such as from finish to start. Examine souvenirs, mementos, photos, or any materials associated with the event. Consult someone else who was present. Ask that person questions that will elicit a memory. Sometimes a guided recall by someone else is better than interrogating yourself.

Details of parties, vacations, and the like

Registration: As the experience progresses, you can tell if it is to be a memorable one. Think about details on your way home: who attended, what they wore and talked about, what was served. Keep a diary or scrapbook with souvenirs, photos, and recordings that help you relive the event. Reminisce with companions.

Remembering: Imagine yourself back in the experience. Recall the day and what you did just before the special occasion. Consult someone else who was there, and keep him or her talking. (People often think that they don't recall an event, but then it comes back to them as they continue to talk.) Consult photos or other mementos that were saved.

Familiar faces

Registration: Describe the person's face to yourself—mouth shape, nose size and shape, color of eyes, and the character they project. Try to see similarity to other faces familiar to you. Don't be preoccupied with studying someone's facial features, but make judgments about them instead. Who do they remind you of? Do they seem honest, sensitive, interesting? Think of people you know who have a similar face.

Making a judgment about a person will help you remember the name that goes with the face.

Remembering: Reinstate a situation in which you may have met. Sometimes an album or a yearbook will help. If you fail to recognize the person, be blunt about it, but apologetic.

Misplaced files

Registration: Label new files accurately and in a way that will lead you to them immediately when you need them. If you notice that files are out of order, don't file a new folder until the order is corrected. Keep a directory of files on paper or on computer.

Remembering: Go through all files occasionally and reorganize or discard ones that are obsolete. The fewer you have to go through, the easier it will be to find what you want.

Recalling a first meeting

Registration: If the meeting is planned, decide what will be worth attending and remembering. If you are not alerted to the meeting, decide what is valuable to you

---

Steer your conversation in a direction that will help your memory.

---

as it transpires or immediately afterward; describe it to yourself at the first opportunity and make notes. Talk to others about the meeting right away.

Remembering: Reconstruct the logic of the first meeting: Why were you there? What were the circumstances? What was the result? Look for records that might refer to that first meeting. Engage in conversations that might bring back memories.

Diet details

Registration: Some diets tell what is to be eaten at all times of the day. But other diets leave the choices to you, and it's your responsibility to keep track of what you eat in terms of food groups, calories, grams, or some other unit of measure. One reason these diets may fail is that people often forget what kind and how much of each food they ate. To avoid these pitfalls, spend extra time rehearsing to yourself what you have eaten thus far in the day. You may want to record your intake in a notebook kept next to your place at the table or attached to your refrigerator.

Remembering: Recall what foods you're supposed to eat as part of your diet. This may serve to remind you of what you actually ate at a sitting. Look to your notes for confirmation. If you don't have notes, ask a table companion to help you recall the menu.

Ingredients used in preparing a recipe

Registration: Describe the ingredients to yourself as you lay them out. Make mental or written notes about the ingredients you will use, or do so as you use them.

Discuss the recipe with anyone present while you are preparing things. Reflect on the ingredients already used. Go over the recipe in a cookbook or recipe file.

You can master a recipe without a cookbook.

Remembering: Practice recalling all of the ingredients the dish calls for. Mentally recreate the sequence in which you used the ingredients. Reenact your preparation, trying to recall the different spots in the kitchen where you used each ingredient. Ask someone who was present to question you about which ingredients you used, to guide you through the retrieval process. Check for sensory detail—real memories tend to have more details than imagined ones.

Money or objects you lend

Registration: When you lend something, ask the person when it will be returned. Imagine yourself handing the person money. Associate the loan with other events of the day and with anyone who might have been present. Associate the loan with the date it is to be paid back. Keep accurate records: Note on your calendar and appointment book when the loan is due, and when you should ask for its return.

When it comes to lending money or belongings, it pays to be organized.

Remembering: Check your records periodically to remind yourself of loans you have recorded. If you have a feeling that someone owes you something, though it's not written down, take some guesses based on past lending experiences. Look around to see what's missing and try to pinpoint a likely borrower.

Missing keys

Registration: Put your keys in one regular spot all the time: a key rack, special pocket, or bowl by the door. Get in the habit of checking the lock to make sure you don't leave the key in it when you leave or enter. Pat your pockets if you keep your keys on your person, or occasionally check the place where you normally carry them. Keep your keys on a string, chain, or other device that attaches to clothing.

Remembering: Retrace your steps. Check all places where you normally leave your keys. Try to recall any distractions on your way to where you usually put your keys. Check outerwear pockets.

Misplaced object

Registration: Have a routine for the way you lay things out. It may seem boring, but sometimes a little boredom is the price we have to pay to keep our sanity. Consistent placement habits make it easier to find things later. Use object organizers at every opportunity. If you can't find something, be methodical—go step by step. Be aware of who is around while you do a task so you can consult them later if necessary. Before you have a chance to lose things, make an object check—see that everything is where you intended it to be. Take objects with you, if possible.

Remembering: Recall what you were doing just before you misplaced the object. Think of the last time you remember holding the object. Be logical—if you just walked in the house and you can't find your purse, you know it's not at the office—or you wouldn't have been able to pay your bus fare or use your house key. Retrace your steps. Think of when you used the object last. Check object organizers and standard places. Clear the area where the object disappeared.

You can find what you're looking for by using a little logic.

Long-lost objects

Registration: When you put something down, mentally rehearse the name of the object with its location. Imagine the object in the location. Imagine returning and finding the object. Put objects in expected and orderly places. Keep a place for priority items. Label your storage closets and cabinets. Go through the basement or storage area periodically and check to see that things are where they are supposed to be.

Remembering: Recall the last time you used the item. Go to places where you probably used it. Remember ways you found the object in the past. Make sure you haven't loaned the object to anyone or that someone did not move it or put it back in an unfamiliar place. If you blame someone else for losing the object, he or she will probably help you find it just to prove you wrong. If all else fails, go through all of your possessions. You may be lucky and find something else that was missing.

Your parked car's location

Registration: Attend carefully the moment you park your car. Notice buildings, stores, adjacent parked cars, or other landmarks. Repeat the name of the street or position of the car several times before leaving it. Remember the route that you take from the car to your destination. Try to park near an obvious landmark. Put a distinctive flag on your antenna or a sticker on your bumper. Leave something prominent in the windshield. If you are unsure, write the location down or sketch a map. If the car is rented or borrowed, note the car's make, color, and license plate number.

Observe the environment around your car before leaving it in a crowded parking lot or on a city street.

Remembering: Reconstruct an image of the spot where the car was parked. Think of stores, buildings, and mall entrances you passed after you left the car. Try to retrace your steps. Return to the car by the original route you used.

Long statements, questions, or requests

Registration: Don't try to take in everything that is said. Instead, pay attention to key words and rehearse them. Restate the question in your own terms or ask the questioner to paraphrase it in brief terms. Pay extra attention to people given to making long utterances, or to situations where long questions often occur (such as in court or in a lecture). Use a notepad when possible.

Remembering: Acknowledge that the statement was long. Tell the other party that you can't cover *all* that was mentioned, but you will address the most important points. Then respond to whatever you recall of your key terms. As you speak, watch the faces in your audience to determine if you might have missed anything. Ask if you covered everything satisfactorily. If you didn't, have your questioner repeat any points you missed.

Messages received when you're sleepy

Registration: Think about the importance of the message. If it is a high priority, give it more of your serious attention. Just rating the information as important will cause it to be remembered better. Shorten the message to one key word and remember that. Make a note on a pad next to your bed. Ask the person giving you the message to leave a note for you. Make a game of it—have both of you try to remember the message and see who will be the first to mention it in the morning.

Remembering just one key word will help you remember the whole message.

Remembering: Check your bedside notepad. Try to retrieve your key word and reconstruct the message from that. Punch in your sense of urgency on the matter to jog your memory.

Names of people introduced to you

Registration: Prime yourself ahead of time by asking who you might be meeting. If you have at least heard the name before being introduced, half the battle is won. Arrive before most of the guests. By doing this, you won't have to meet everyone at the same time, so you have more of an opportunity to learn the names and faces.

Use the three-point face-name imagery technique:

1. Think of a word that reminds you of the person's last name. As an example, when you are introduced to Mr. Donaldson, think of Donald Duck.
2. Select the most outstanding feature of the person's face, such as Mr. Donaldson's nose.
3. Form an image of your substitute word (*duck*) on the person's face.

You might also try the four-point SALT method:

1. *Say* the name out loud.
2. *Ask* the person a question using his or her name.
3. *(At) Least* once, use the name in conversation.
4. *Terminate* the conversation by using the name again.

Remember names by thinking of SALT: say, ask, at least, terminate.

Other techniques: Think of a rhyme for the name. Think of a friend or celebrity the person looks like. Translate the name into another language. Note the person's eccentricities. Analyze the national/ethnic origins of the name.

When you leave the situation, think back and try to recall the names of people you met. Think of what they looked like. Pronounce their names aloud. Jot down the names at your earliest opportunity. This is especially helpful when you encounter several introductions in a row on a receiving line. Talk about who you met with others. It's considered socially acceptable to ask someone his or her name after just being introduced in a situation that is hurried and hectic. In fact, it may even be regarded as a compliment because you appear to consider the person's name worth knowing. Imagine settings in which you might encounter these new people in the future. Imagine meeting them and saying their names in this setting.

Remembering: Recall when and where you met this person and how you felt at the time. Visualize the person for physical reminders. Think of the number of syllables or unusual letters in the name. Go through the alphabet letter by letter and try to retrieve the first letter of the name. Try for national or ethnic clues. Ask the person whose name you want to remember how to pronounce the name, so you get the answer without having to admit forgetting it. (You'll look pretty silly, however, if the name is Jones.) Refer to notes, an address book, or programs to social functions. Check the directory of names that is often displayed on the first floor of office buildings. If all hope is lost, avoid referring to the person by name.

Names of old acquaintances

Registration: Reminisce with others about mutual friends from the past as a way to refresh your memory for their names in a context. When you hear others mention a familiar name from long ago, say the name to yourself; rhyme it with other names you know.

Remembering: Try to gather enough information to spark your memory. Ask, "What have you been doing all these years?" If you have a mutual acquaintance, ask, "Whatever happened to _____? Where is he now?" Inquire about the person's work. Look for monograms on handkerchiefs, ties, purses, and clothing.

Asking the right pointed questions can help get you out of an embarrassing situation fast.

Names of people in a receiving line

Registration: Repeat each name to yourself, and also say it aloud. Cluster similar names together or make a rhyme. Use the method of loci or the peg system. Pay attention to faces. Mentally review the line and jot down the names as soon as you get the chance. Remember to *make the effort.* It is all too easy to go down a line shaking hands and being quite personable, without even *trying* to learn any of the names.

Remembering: Try to picture the line and who was next to the person whose name you want to recall. Retrieve the person from his or her peg. Go through the alphabet, searching for the first letter. Ask a question that might ring a bell.

What food and drinks you have served to whom at a social occasion

Registration: It sounds silly, but it often works: Imagine those who have been served as having an *X* on their nose. Give out a napkin for each drink you serve. Review your orders repeatedly.

Remembering: Try to recall those of your guests you "marked" with an *X* on their nose. Notice what kinds of plates or glasses they have.

Remember drink orders by the shape of the glass.

Photos: time, place, subjects, and photographer

Registration: Look at your photos carefully after they are processed and attempt to remember as much as you can about them. Immediately write these details on the back of each one.

Remembering: Periodically, look over the photos and refresh your memory. Check for a date and an event on the back. If there is none, try to identify the event and the people shown by linking them together in your memory at a picnic, dinner, wedding, or holiday, for example.

Their clothes and age may help to identify the date and the event.

Places visited on a trip

Registration: Before going on the trip, memorize the key stops. As you depart from each place, rehearse its name and link it with the name of the previous stop. Pay attention to your surroundings. Keep a diary and take photos during the trip. Test yourself along the way.

Remembering: Retrace the trip in your mind. Reminisce about the trip with others. Imagine the place as it was when you first visited there. Think of the time frame in terms of other contemporary events. Look at your diary, mementos, or souvenirs.

Views you expressed on an issue

Registration: Pay attention to all points of view expressed, especially on controversial issues. Keep track of other people's positions as well as your own in conversations. In formal situations, take notes or use recording devices.

Remembering: Think of previous positions you have taken on other issues. Reconstruct your most likely position. Think carefully. Let the other party begin the

---

Encourage others to do all the talking so you can give yourself time to think.

discussion, giving you time to think. Steer the conversation in a way that elicits cues.

Contents of personal correspondence

Registration: Save your correspondence, especially important letters. Keep it organized, so you can do a memory check easily at any time. Read short letters twice, or more often if they are important. Make copies of important letters you have written before you send them. File the copies carefully. Read your own letters over before putting them in an envelope.

Remembering: Recall the purpose of the letter. Reconstruct what you would say if you had to write the letter again. Look at letters you received and any copies you have of those you wrote.

What you said to whom

Registration: Create a mental list when you inform people of something. In business, it is wise to keep notes about content and participants in important conversations.

Remembering: Recall the situation and your mood. Go "fishing" for indications by bringing up the subject and seeing if the other person has a recollection that you discussed it. Check your notes.

In business, it is important to keep notes on people you meet. You can impress them later by recalling unusual facts.

Intentions

Routine tasks before leaving the house

Registration: Do these things in the same sequence and at the same time every day. Lay out utensils and tools the night before or ahead of time. Put them by the front door or in some other place you are sure to see before walking out.

Remembering: Run through your routine in your mind when you awake. Then tick off accomplished tasks and keep reviewing what remains to be done at significant junctures—when leaving the bathroom, when going to breakfast, when leaving the house.

A new routine to follow

Registration: Write out your entire schedule for the first few days. Prioritize. Deliberately establish important times on the schedule in your mind. Put objects in unusual places to remind you of things. Use alarms. Consult notes.

Remembering: Review the parts of the new routine before you go to sleep and upon awakening. Discuss your new duties with others and talk about how you organize the jobs.

Appointments and meetings

Registration: Imagine yourself going to the place of the appointment at the appropriate time. Imagine what you will be doing just before the appointment and associ-

---

Use the time spent falling asleep at night as review time.

---

ate that activity with the appointment to follow. Imagine the face of your watch set to the time of the appointment alongside a symbol representing it (such as a piggy bank to remind you of a trip to the bank, or a shopping cart for the supermarket). Sketch or diagram what you are to do. Imagine the good that will come by keeping the appointment. Imagine the consequences of failing to do so.

Remembering: Keep a record of the things you have to do habitually (on an appointment book, calendar, diary, or bulletin board). Transfer notes about new appointments into your appointment book as soon as possible. Use a two-tier system: a calendar that keeps all long- and short-range intentions and an appointment book with the same information plus any last-minute meetings. Review your schedule at least twice a day—once at night to make sure your plans are workable and once in the morning to energize them in your mind. Use alarms. If you are rushed and don't have time to jot down an appointment, change your environment in some obvious way: Tip a lampshade, switch your watch to the other wrist, or put something on the floor in a conspicuous place. Make notes about meetings immediately after arranging them.

Two appointment books are better than one.

Cards and gifts to be sent

Registration: Associate the date with some other event that precedes it. Record birthdays in your address book as soon as you find out about them. Transfer the date onto your calendar, and keep the calendar in a conspicuous spot. Post memos to yourself. At the beginning of the year, purchase cards for everyone you normally send them to, then address and sign all the cards at once. File them appropriately in an organizer divided into 12 months and be certain to check it on a particular day every month.

Remembering: Glance at the next month on your calendar occasionally to see what birthdays are coming up. Bring birthdays into the conversation with family and close friends.

Taking your change after a purchase

Registration: Remind yourself that you must have two things before you walk away from the counter: your change and the thing you bought. Don't put your wallet or purse away until you've received your change. Hold it in your hand. Make the effort to count your change.

One purchase gives you two *things to carry: the new item and your change.*

Remembering: Keep your wallet or purse in hand until you receive your change. Before leaving the store, make it a habit to check your change to be sure it's correct.

Necessary chores

Registration: Put tools for the particular chore in a conspicuous place. If your vacuum cleaner is in the closet, it's easy to forget you need to use it. If it's in the middle of the floor, you'll certainly remember. Avoid being distracted from your chores. Use notes, calendars, a memo board, or alarms.

Remembering: Mentally run down a checklist of chores at home or office once a day to jog your memory for duties left undone.

Unpleasant Tasks

Registration: Prioritize. Remind yourself with increasing frequency as the time of action approaches. Set an alarm. Set *another* alarm. Place notes to yourself in conspicuous places. Think of the consequences if you forget. Promise yourself a reward when the task is done.

Remembering: Think through a litany of chores that bore or annoy you, to see if the missing one pops up. Ask friends or family about your distasteful jobs that they see undone.

You can pick up a conversation after being distracted and no one will ever know you strayed.

Turning off the range or oven

Registration: Organize your cooking to make it less hectic, minimizing the chance that you will forget any steps. Determine the duration of time the dish will take to cook and plan an activity that fills the same time. (For instance, if you have to turn the oven off in 15 minutes, put on a record album. When one side is finished playing, time is up.) Set timers.

Remembering: Pay strict attention to your matching activity's conclusion or to any alarms you set. Respond immediately, lest you forget!

Correspondence due

Registration: As soon as you decide that correspondence should be sent, make a note on your calendar and in your appointment book regarding its content. There is computer software that will sound an alarm on preset dates, and this can be used to remind yourself to take care of important correspondence.

Remembering: Check your calendar, appointment book, or other external aid regularly. Unless you have a secretary whose job responsibility includes reminding you of things, be wary of depending on others. They may forget, too.

Low-priority deadlines

Registration: Low priority deadlines are difficult to remember because we don't register them well in the first place. Be certain to write them down in your schedule and review it daily. Imagine doing something that immediately precedes the deadline, and associate it with the deadline. Then, when you perform the associated act, it will tend to evoke the deadline in your mind.

Low priority items are impossible to remember without the aid of a mental manipulation.

Remembering: Exact deadline tasks which must be performed by a specific time invite the use of external memory aids like alarm watches. Check your calendar daily for any approaching deadlines.

Serving all the dishes you prepared for a meal

Registration: Plan and prepare as much of the meal ahead of time as possible. Write down the planned menu and the order for serving it. Revise it as required until mealtime.

Remembering: Make it a point to do a once-over through the kitchen before sitting down to eat. Follow your written aids.

Buttons, zippers, and accessories

Registration: Put on your clothes in an organized manner, such as from the top down or from the bottom up. Lay out your clothing and accessories for the next day in advance. Try to leave yourself enough time so you don't have to rush to put your clothes on.

Remembering: Look in a mirror before leaving the house and examine yourself from head to toe. If you discover something is unfastened, check that item specially for the next few days; people tend to repeat that same error for several days due to fatigue or stress.

Errands

Registration: Prioritize your errands. Note how many things you need to do or buy. If possible, do an errand as soon as you realize it needs to be done. The longer you wait, the greater the chance the memory trace will fade or disappear entirely. Prepare a detailed to-do list and take it with you when you go out. Carry one of your tools, utensils, or materials related to the errand with you.

Remembering: Cross errands off your to-do list as soon as you complete them, glancing at the remaining ones as an on-going reminder. Browse through the store, glancing at the products on shelves that might serve as reminders.

Always note the number of items on your list. It's an easy way to find out if you're missing something.

What you're looking for in a room

Registration: When you set out to look for something in another room, mention it to someone as you go. If you're alone, say why you're going out loud to yourself.

Picture it in your mind; think of what you'll do with the object when you get it.

Remembering: Look around for clues. Return to the place where the intention was formed and look for clues that might tip off what prompted you to go in the room. Think of the last thing you were doing. Don't trouble yourself over it, because as the cliche goes, "If you forgot it, it must not have been that important to begin with."

Information given in a hectic situation

Registration: Repeat the message to the source. Get the source to repeat the message to you ("No, really?" "How is that?" "Come again?"). Ask the source to mention it again later, when things aren't so hectic. Write the message down at your first opportunity. Turn your watch face down on your wrist or switch it to the other wrist to remind you to write the message down later. Set an alarm to remind you to write it down later. Rehearse the message mentally until you have the chance to record it on a reliable memory aid. Note the importance of the source—you may decide to ignore the message.

Remembering: Mentally repeat the message, seeing yourself as you received it—what the speaker looked like, where you were, and why the message seemed important.

In stressful and hectic situations, repeat an important message over and over.

Try to recall some of the words used—even a few will often cue you to the topic of the message.

Taking your keys with you

Registration: Put your keys in one consistent take-away spot by the door. Develop a "pat your pocket" ritual before closing the door. Hold onto your keys whenever you take them out. Put something in the doorway (such as a briefcase, purse, or your foot) and don't remove it until you have the key in your hand. Put a lock on your door that will not lock unless you turn the key in it. Leave a key with a trusted friend or neighbor.

Remembering: Retrace your steps. Look in all the usual places you put your keys, plus the places where they might have slipped out of sight (under a chair cushion or off the edge of a table).

Maintenance of your car and household appliances

Registration: Keep a logbook on your possessions, indicating when they require maintenance. Mark the maintenance schedule on your calendar along with your other appointments and obligations. Tag your possessions with the date of their last service.

Remembering: Check your log or appointment book weekly or monthly for maintenance cues.

Medication as scheduled

Registration: Imagine a clock with a pill at each hour that medication is to be taken. Get a pillbox with

---

Log books are indispensable when it comes to keeping track of personal belongings.

---

separate compartments representing the hours in a day or days in a week. There are even pillboxes with alarms that can be set to go off at the time you need to take medication. Have your spouse, friend, or nurse help you keep track of these times.

One strategy is to put the exact number of pills you need to take in a dish or pillbox at the beginning of the day. If there are too many pills in the box at a certain time, you know you missed one. If the pills are all gone, you know you have taken them all. However, this strategy is not advised for people whose pills must be taken at a precise time.

Remembering: Review your medication schedule each time you take medication. If you think you missed a medication, reconstruct how you spent your time during the day—it may remind you of when you took the medication in question. If you're still in doubt, call your doctor rather than risk the consequences of an overdose.

Packing essentials for a trip

Preparation: Lay your suitcase out a few days before the trip and toss in things you want to take along as you come across them. That way, you don't have to remember them all at the last minute.

Remembering: Look at each part of your body and pick out the necessary clothes for every day of the trip.

Start from the top down or the bottom up to make sure you don't leave anything out. Make a checklist of items you always take on trips. Ask someone else going on the trip what he or she is taking along. When you think you are finished packing, consider unusual things that are easily forgotten—raingear, toiletries, camera, and such. Pack at a leisurely pace, and well in advance. Don't wait until it's time to go to the airport.

Never save packing for the last minute. You're bound to forget something.

Taking what you brought (and bought) back home

Registration: Only unpack those things that are necessary—in other words, "live out of a suitcase." Keep dirty clothes in a bag near your suitcase.

Remembering: Imagine parts of your body and clothes for those parts. Make a checklist of things you purchased, and go over it before packing. Systematically go through every drawer and closet. After you have packed the suitcases and placed them outside your room, go back inside and check one last time. Ask someone to interview you about which things you may have left behind.

Paying your bills on time

Registration: Keep unpaid bills in a visible place. Note the due dates of bills on your calendar, and review it every day. Make one particular day of the month your bill-paying day. In fact, it may help to make one day of the month your "memory day." Reserve that day for paying bills, servicing the car, and doing other easily forgotten tasks.

Make one day a month your memory day for doing those easy-to-forget tasks.

Remembering: Review your bills at least twice a month. Use external aids (tipped lampshades, overturned wastebasket, bills in your pen clip) as reminders.

Making necessary phone calls

Registration: Imagine yourself standing by a phone next to a clock with the hands set to the time the call is to be made. Put a note about the call in your appointment book, and review it several times each day. Leave a note about the call in a visible place. Some automatic dialing systems have the capability to alert you when a call is to be made. Set a watch alarm or a wind-up kitchen timer.

Leave notes for yourself on your telephone. That way you won't leave callers waiting.

Remembering: Check your notebook regularly for calls you have to make. If you have a feeling that you owe a call, pursue it by thinking of people who called you recently—it may remind you of a call you owe.

Returning library books

Registration: Write return dates on your calendar as soon as you bring the books home. As the due date approaches, place the books by your front door or in some other regular take-away spot. Consider the consequences of not returning the books.

Remembering: Make returning library books one of your routine chores. Tie it to stopping for gas or shopping for groceries.

Resetting clocks for seasonal time changes

Registration: Indicate on your calendar the Sunday in the spring and fall when the clocks have to changed. Remember the saying, "spring forward, fall back."

Remembering: When you hear or read announcements of the upcoming time change, make a note on your calendar or, if it's just a few days away, put your alarm clock in an obvious and unusual place.

New ideas with no time to make notes

Registration: During the conversation, associate the idea with something you will do later. Mentally rehearse the idea several times after you first think of it, even if that means you contribute little or nothing to the conversation. Keep pads of paper or index cards on your person or at least handy. Write the idea down as soon as you can. Change the physical environment in some way (turn a ring, switch your watch to the other wrist, or position something oddly on your desk) or set an alarm on your watch to remind you to make a note later.

Remembering: If you have a feeling of knowing, think of the first letter, number of syllables, or images of the idea. Brainstorm periodically to recall ideas you forgot.

Important thoughts during sleep time

Registration: Turn the idea over in your mind a few times before going back to sleep. Position something oddly on your night table so you'll be reminded in the morning that there was something you wanted to remember. Keep a notepad at your bedside.

Keep a notepad and pencil by your bedside to jot down those great ideas that hit you in the middle of the night.

Remembering: If you feel you had an important thought, try to recall the first letter or syllables of key words in the thought. Also, try to think of any dreams that might be related or topics that crossed your mind before bedtime.

Starting on time

Registration: Prioritize the task. Associate the event with other events that immediately precede it. Imagine a large clock with the hands set to the starting time and yourself about to begin the action. Remind yourself with increasing frequency as the starting time approaches. Set alarms or timers.

Remembering: Recall the time for the task and time for any activity that precedes it. Say the time and the action to yourself repeatedly during the interval. Ignore any interruptions. If you use an alarm, act immediately when it goes off.

Turning off lights when you leave a room

Registration: Think of all the things you will be doing before it's time to leave the room, then determine which one is likely to occur *just before* you go. Link that action to flicking the light switch, so they combine into a single action in your mind.

Remembering: Pay particular attention to the "off" position when you turn on a light. Make a mental note to use it before you leave the room. Think of a light bulb in the shape of a dollar sign.

Getting up on time

Registration: Rehearse the reason for your special intention to be up on time. ("I must be up early to get to the bank before going to work.") That helps you remember to set *two* alarm clocks. Put one under the bed or in some other unusual place, and put the second alarm across the room so that you have to get out of bed to turn it off.

Remembering: Think of the consequences of failing to get up. ("I won't have money for gas if I don't get to the bank.") Force yourself to jump out of bed the instant you awake and think of the reason you're up so early—the bank!

Set two alarms for those times when you absolutely must be there first thing in the morning.

Actions

Activity just interrupted

Preparation: When you stop in the middle of doing something, go over in your mind what you still have left to do. Mentally repeat the name of the action, and then the word "done" on completing the action. Imagine yourself performing the action, and keep repeating your intention to do so. Link the action to some aspect of where you are so the context will remind you of it. Do specific actions on specific days. Watch others and imitate them. Realize what you are doing is important, and concentrate on it throughout the day.

Remembering: Look at your surroundings—sometimes they will trigger what you were doing. Retrace steps. Jot down ahead of time what you need to do during the day and then refer to the note. Use a checklist.

Performing a familiar action correctly

Registration: Develop new ways to do redundant actions. Practice actions you want to perfect long enough to have them down pat. Become aware of possible errors that may occur in doing an action so you can watch out for them. Rent how-to videotapes to refresh your memory for some actions, such as playing sports.

Remembering: Pause before you do the act, and think of the steps. Don't attempt the task if you are tired or too busy. Pay close attention to what you are doing, because you may be a little rusty. Ask someone who can perform the action correctly to demonstrate it before attempting it yourself.

Don't attempt to duplicate a perfect action when you are tired or too busy. The results will be disappointing.

Completing ordinary actions

Registration: Mentally rehearse completion of the act, (removing the key from the lock, taking the clothes from the dryer) and double check your actions. Mentally talk yourself through the action. Do things methodically— by the numbers, step by step. Set timers or alarms if appropriate.

Remembering: Get into good "end" habits: Before you slam the car door shut, make sure the key is out of the lock and on your person. When you go inside the house, make sure you put the door key in a particular spot.

Proper form in a sport

Registration: Imitate the correct form with the assistance of a coach, book, photograph, or video. Break the movement down into smaller components. Mentally rehearse the movement during idle moments (such as during a bus ride or while waiting for a friend). Practice as often as you can.

Remembering: Remind yourself of previous errors in form and the remedies you discovered. Take as much time as you need warming up and practicing the movement.

All necessary stops while running errands

Registration: Before you start out, imagine the destination and the route. (Plan a route that takes you by the necessary stops in order.) Put a note or something meaningful on the dashboard to remind you (for the bank, checks or deposit slips; for the supermarket, coupons).

When setting out to do several errands, plan a route that takes you to the necessary stops in sequence.

Remembering: Reconstruct what you were doing just before you left the house and review any plans you made for the trip. Check the contents of the car for clues to stops you might have missed. If you have a passenger, discuss the errand.

Getting gas and oil on time

Registration: Although most cars these days flash a warning light when gas and/or oil is low, people still run out of both for one of two reasons: They ignore the warning lights and forget to fill up later, or they forget to plan a stop where service stations are available. You can save yourself by routinely seeking a service station whenever the gas supply is less than half a tank and checking your oil when you get the gas. When you're on a trip, plan ahead by filling up before you head into a desolate stretch.

Remembering: Respond to the warning light by servicing your car at once!

Replacing the gas cap after a self-service fill-up

Registration: Always tell yourself, as you remove the cap, "Many people forget to replace the cap, and I must avoid that mistake." Make it a habit to put the cap in the same conspicuous place (on the fender or on the trunk lid just above the gas receptacle is best—never on the roof where it's out of sight and easy to forget) while the gas is flowing. If this is a recurring problem for you, position a memo on the dash reminding you to replace the cap; buy a wire, chain, or other device that connects the gas cap to the car.

Remembering: Write the memo for the dash. Develop the habit of not leaving the station unless you can recall replacing the cap. Ask your passengers to quiz you about it.

Turning off high beams and turn signals

Registration: Keep your finger on the lever or button while these signals are activated. Remind yourself that these actions are "starters" and must be followed by "enders."

Remembering: Check your high beams whenever traffic approaches you at night. If someone flashes high beams at you, check yours.

Turning off headlights before you leave the car

Preparation: Walk around the front of your car every time you get out of it. The light on your body should remind you that you forgot something. Turn off the car methodically—lights, heat, air conditioning, wipers, engine. Some cars (most notably, Saabs) turn off their electrical system automatically when the engine is shut off.

Make it a habit to pass in front of your car every time you get out, and you'll never forget to turn off your headlights.

Remembering: Routinely check to be sure all controls on the car have been set properly before getting out of it. If you get out with packages and notice the lights are still on, don't take the bundles into the house first, intending to come back. You might forget to do so!

Locking car keys in your car

Registration: Some cars cannot be locked without using a key to do it. That's virtually foolproof, but not universal. Many cars remind you with a buzzer or a bell if you try to exit the car while the keys are in the ignition. Resolve to remove the keys immediately when you hear it, otherwise you may join the hordes who tune the sound out and lock the keys in. Also, make it a point to put the keys right in your pocket or purse when you remove them. Some people put the keys on the front seat or the dash as they collect their belongings before leaving the car. Then as they slam the door they spot the keys on the seat, locked inside.

Remembering: Remove the keys as soon as you arrive at your destination and put them with other belongings you will take along. Train yourself to check for your keys before you shut your car door. And just in case, carry a spare set of keys.

Proper etiquette

Registration: Review potential etiquette situations before events (opening a door, pulling out a chair, someone's handing you something, someone's holding your coat, someone's bumping into you, awkward pauses in conversation). Do a quick rehearsal so you will remember proper behavior (which fork to use, how to make introductions, and so forth). Anticipate the beginnings and endings to events where etiquette is critical. Discuss local customs with a native. Make politeness habitual. Examine an etiquette book. Be sensitive to situations in which you might say or do the wrong thing. When you make a faux pas or see someone else do so, make a mental note of it, so history won't repeat itself in your case.

Rehearse the polite behavior expected of you before you step out into new company.

Remembering: Check on your repeated errors in etiquette. Browse through etiquette books periodically. Read newspaper columns on etiquette. Remind yourself of the level of etiquette called for by a situation. Take your lead from others who know.

A step in a sequence

Registration: Many situations require that you hear or read a set of instructions, then execute steps in a certain order. For example, a carpenter makes cabinets according to a sequence of specified steps. Failure to recall a step or failure to execute the proper steps in order can ruin the results. To prevent such forgetting, take a moment to imagine each stage of a multi-faceted task from start to finish. When time allows, associate each step with the next one either verbally or with interactive imagery.

When setting out on a complicated task, review each step visually in your head before acting on it and going on to the next step.

Remembering: As you perform a sequence, take care to finish each step completely before moving on to the next one. Set aside objects associated with each step (such as items to be used in making a project) so that a glance at them will remind you of where you are in the sequence. Notice which steps are already done and review them frequently.

Embarrassing slips in conversation

Registration: Be aware of which subjects are taboo among your friends or colleagues. Avoid conversations involving sensitive topics where you might make a slip. Search your memory for previous unfortunate experiences as clues to potential errors you want to guard against.

Remembering: When you have made a slip of the tongue, be aware of it and its related content so you will be less likely to do it again. If you make a lot of embarrassing slips, remain silent long enough to reflect on any possible offense your next comment could convey.

The More the Merrier

A lot of memory situations were covered in this chapter, but it would be impossible to cover every single memory problem you might encounter in your life. If a situation you have in mind is not included here, look for those that are similar. You may be able to adapt one of them to your particular problem.

You won't always be able to use a task-specific manipulation. For incidental memory tasks (which you execute without being aware you're performing a memory task), the general mental manipulations you learned in chapter 6 are necessary. But if there is the possibility of using a strategy that is specific to a particular situation, by all means use it.

Use two, if you can. The more manipulations you use, the better. Consider the situation of having to learn someone's name. One technique is to pay attention to the name's ethnic roots. Another is to analyze the name's length and unusual combinations of letters. These two different techniques clearly emphasize different aspects of the same task.

You meet four men: Mr. Jones, Mr. Malloy, Mr. Armstrong, and Mr. Andrzejewski. To many Americans, *Jones* is a neutral name, because its ethnic roots are obscure and its spelling is typical. *Malloy* also has a commonplace spelling, but we recognize it as Irish. *Armstrong*, like *Jones*, is ethnically neutral, but the name combines two common words in a distinct, fairly ordinary way. *Andrzejewski* is ethnically interesting and identifiable for its Polish roots, and its spelling is unusual in both length and letter combinations.

If you attend to the ethnic roots of these four names, it becomes more memorable from *Jones* and *Armstrong* to *Malloy* and *Andrzejewski*. If you pay attention to the letters and sounds, it becomes more memorable from *Jones* and *Malloy* to *Armstrong* and *Andrzejewski*. Only *Andrzejewski* draws a maximum reaction from both techniques.

The point is that each of these manipulations can be used to learn the names, but not with the same effect. The most effective technique would be to use both manipulations, and perhaps a third or fourth if they are appropriate. Using many manipulations allows each one to make up for any loss in effectiveness of the others. Plus, using two or more manipulations ensures that you will pay extra attention to what you want to remember, making success more likely.

The more mental manipulations you use, the greater your success will be at mastering a task.

Now don't try to memorize every manipulation in this chapter. That will actually lead to *worse* memory performance. Begin with just one or two memory situations that seriously annoy you and that you consider especially important. If you can improve your performance on them, you will have worked on something that most genuinely matters to you. Later, you can pick other tasks and try those manipulations.

The techniques in this chapter require practice to be useful. Obviously, the *difficulty level* of a particular strategy will influence whether or not you use it. Generally, more difficult manipulations produce a better memory trace. But if your time is limited, you may want to pick an easier manipulation.

When you decide which manipulations you'd like to try, I'd suggest you write the name of the task on one side of a small card and the manipulation on the other. Leave the card in a prominent spot, such as next to your bed or on your desk at work. Each time you notice the card, try to recall the manipulation. With practice, you should be able to remember it automatically every time you think of the task.

Summary

Techniques that help you conquer specific memory tasks give you an advantage because they prepare you for the jobs in advance. The techniques in this chapter address over 100 situations that people rate most troubling. Whenever possible, you should use a technique that is geared for a particular memory situation.

Chapter 9

MEMORY SAVVY: MEETING YOUR POTENTIAL

The final step in a complete approach to memory improvement is to develop your *memory savvy*. That means you must learn to recognize your own memory problems, link them with the right remedial techniques, and apply those techniques to the appropriate memory situations.

Right Place, Right Time

A memory technique is virtually useless if you implement it at the wrong time. To know if a particular mental manipulation should be used in a given situation, ask yourself two key questions:

1. *Does the manipulation fit the memory situation?* When some people draw up a food shopping list, they're *thinking* of the meals they plan to cook and the ingredients that are required to make each recipe. To those who don't actually cook, on the other hand, such a shopping list might seem like a collection of unconnected words with no obvious purpose. The first person might mem-

orize a shopping list best by concentrating on the *meaning* of the items, while the second person would probably be better off silently rehearsing the *pronunciation* of the items. It's counterproductive to use a mental manipulation that isn't compatible with the memory situation.

2. *Does the manipulation require more effort than the situation warrants?* If you're doing a week's grocery shopping, you could memorize your 50-item shopping list using flash cards, spaced rehearsal, method of loci, and other mental schemes. But it would be a lot quicker and easier to simply jot down the list on a scrap of paper and head for the supermarket. It would be silly to devote so much mental energy to a task that suits itself to a simple external memory aid.

Ask yourself if the memory task you're about to undertake is worth the effort before you begin the exercise.

On the other hand, if you have a big exam or meeting coming up and it calls for reciting a vital list by heart, the smart thing is to devote the time and effort to using the most powerful mental manipulations available and fusing that information solidly into your long-term memory.

To answer these two questions correctly in *any* memory situation, it's important to blend your knowledge about your own skills and inclinations with a clear understanding of your targeted memory tasks and the techniques you could apply to them. The trick is to assess the current memory situation accurately and choose a mental manipulation from those in the previous chapters that fits it best.

The simplest way to see if you're using the right memory techniques is to evaluate how well they've served you. You probably don't notice when your memory is succeeding, but when you have a memory *failure*, it's a good time to figure out what's going on.

You must evaluate your progress routinely to make sure that what you're doing is really working.

The next time you lock your keys in the car or can't remember the name of someone you just met, don't curse yourself and move on to your next responsibility. Stop and ask yourself: What went wrong? What adjustment could I make in registering that information next time that would enable me to succeed at the task?

If you're serious about improving your memory, self-observation can be conducted in a more systematic fashion. A memory diary with a checklist of tasks gives you information about your current successes and failures at memory, making it easier to target tasks that deserve more effort. Even if you don't keep formal records, you might routinely review your recent memory performance.

Controlling Bad Habits

To keep your memory in shape on a regular basis, you should maintain good memory habits and avoid bad ones that can hinder your performance. To see if you've been slipping into bad habits, take the quiz below and indicate how often you act in the manner described.

Checklist for Bad Memory Habits

In the space provided, assign a value to each statement according to this scale:

1-Always   **5-Now and then**
2-Very often   **6-Once in a while**
3-Fairly often   **7-Never**
4-About half the time

1. I hold memory tasks in low regard. _____

2. I hold my own memory ability in low regard. _____

3. I disregard my physical condition, because I assume it won't hinder my memory performance. _____

4. I use adverse substances when performing or when about to perform memory tasks. _____

5. I live an excessively busy lifestyle. _____

6. I live an excessively routine lifestyle. _____

7. I don't make a daily schedule. _____

8. I keep my possessions in a disorganized state. _____

9. I don't use mental manipulations or external memory aids because I expect to remember things without added effort. _____

10. I study while watching TV or while other people are around. _____

11. I study things as a whole, without selecting the main points for greater concentration. _____

12. I let my thoughts wander when I should be learning. _____

13. I go through the motions of learning even though I know my mind is elsewhere. _____

14. I "cram" rather than have a series of study sessions. _____

15. I repeatedly check whether I have done or remembered something even when I remember just making such a check. _____

Your score is calculated by adding the values of responses that you assigned and dividing the sum by the number of statements (15). The score varies depending on a person's age and background, but a typical score would be between 4 and 6. If your score is closer to 2 or 3 and you checked off a lot of "Very oftens," this is a signal that you need to work on reversing those bad habits before you can improve your memory.

Developing Your Memory "Street Smarts"

Superior memory skill requires that you recognize memory situations when you encounter them and use the most appropriate mental manipulations. In other words, develop a sense of memory "street smarts." Whether you're registering information during learning or retrieving it during remembering, you can take steps to organize and check your efforts. These street smarts techniques will help you use memory aids and practices as efficiently as possible.

Imprinting What You Learn

Take advantage of these surefire systems when imprinting information:

● Make sure you're registering the correct information in the first place. Familiarize yourself with everything to be learned before you begin to register information.

Consider whether your learning would be more efficient if you studied the material in parts or as a whole. If you break things into parts in order to learn them, be sure also to spend some time afterwards studying the material as a whole.

Always look for the best method that is also the quickest.

- Whenever possible, use more than one kind of mental manipulation for the same material. This leads to a more durable and accessible memory trace.

    You can usually find a mental manipulation that will increase the strength of the memory trace and one that relates to the attributes of the material. For example, you might learn a list of items by first repeating the words silently, and then by seeing if there are any connections between the items that will make them more meaningful to you.
- Distribute your studying over several sessions. One study session lasting two hours is usually less effective than two one-hour sessions that are separated in time. Study on a schedule, and review periodically after learning.

Two one-hour study sessions are more effective than one two-hour study session.

- Test yourself repeatedly as you learn. Before a study session, estimate how much you will recall. If the material is especially important or detailed, study and test yourself further even after you think you know it 100 percent.

As you test yourself, imagine situations in which you'll be called on to remember the information you learned. Be sensitive to whether you'll be required to recall the information forward or backward. For example, if you're learning French, you should study vocabulary from English-to-French as well as from French-to-English.

Be prepared for plateaus. You'll reach a point where you try as hard as you can, but your recall doesn't seem to improve at all. Just as in tennis or any other sport, plateaus eventually give way to increases in ability.

Simple Tricks for Remembering

You'll be surprised at the effectiveness of these simple tricks:

● Try to recall things at a relaxed pace. Hurrying leads you to miss parts of the information that you really remember. It is also more likely to cause inaccuracies than a slow, deliberate recall. If you don't remember something immediately, don't be ashamed of stalling briefly. Frequently the information will come if you give it a little time.

Recall won't always hit you instantly. Stalling for time gives you the opportunity to collect your thoughts accurately.

● Recall in an optimal order. Chronological order is best, especially when you're trying to recall a story or event.

When the information has been presented recently and quickly, recall the *last* thing you heard *first*, then the *first* thing you heard, and finally try to come up with the information that came in between. When there is a lot of information involved and it's not chronologically organized, break it down into parts. Then, alternate between attempting to recall the parts and the entirety of the material.

- Question yourself. First ask yourself questions that are directly related to specific information you want to remember.

    Then ask yourself about things which relate indirectly to the information. Alternate between direct and indirect questions until your recall succeeds, or until you are convinced that you are blocked.

Mentally edit what you remember before you recall it to others. You can check the correctness of your retrieval in several ways:

- People usually have a reasonably good idea of what they know. Ask yourself how likely you would be to recognize the right answer to a question on the topic. For subjects you know well, your estimate should be high. You should have a lower estimate for unfamiliar subjects. Whether high or low, your estimate is likely to be right more times than not.
- Check the content you have recalled. Does it make sense? Is it internally consistent and plausible? If not, your retrieval may have been flawed. Try to remember again, using other strategies.

You can test the accuracy of your memory by asking yourself four important questions.

- Be sensitive to the fact that you may err in many ways. You might misinterpret the question. You might leave something out.

   A different memory trace might interfere with what you're trying to remember. You might remember at the wrong time (such as remembering an appointment *after* you were due to meet) or in the wrong place. Finally, after retrieving only part of the desired information, you may think you have finished remembering. Double-checking these sources of error can be a way of cross-examining your recall process.

   Screen your recall to be sure you don't blurt out something from memory that may be offensive.

   If your recall efforts fail despite conscientious attempts, give the task a rest. Chances are, the desired item will eventually emerge into consciousness. Try the yoga method of recall. Lie down in a quiet spot where you won't be disturbed. Systematically relax the muscles in your body. When you're extremely relaxed, put questions to yourself about the information you would like to recall.

   If you make the same memory mistake over and over again, take note of it when it happens. Analyze why it happens and figure out a system of steps that you can use the next time the situation arises so the memory failure doesn't happen again.

Keep track of your mistakes in memory. You can analyze them, then correct them.

   Claim an honest level of confidence in the accuracy of your memory. If you know you remember something, say so. If you're wrong, admit it. Everybody makes mistakes.

Give extra scrutiny to answers that come quickly and seem very familiar. Some errors are "strong habits" that intrude upon retrieval.

Practice, Practice, Practice

Research shows that most people can memorize seven consecutive numbers, such as the digits of a telephone number. But with practice, it's possible to recall as many as 80 digits in a row without error! Now, learning lists of numbers is probably not a task you care to excel at, but this dramatic improvement shows how much you stand to gain by vigorously practicing a task of special interest to you.

It's possible to remember 80 digits in a row without an error.

If you know that you're going to encounter a particular memory task regularly, a sure way to get better at it is to practice remembering. Suppose you sell a line of products, for example, and you want to remember the different models perfectly. After you've learned to identify each product type, practice recalling them—without restudying. Then give it a rest and do it again. And again. You'll discover that the speed and number of items you recall will increase.

Typically, a half-dozen repetitions or about 10 minutes per recall are necessary to produce substantial progress. Research indicates that daily attempts over a few weeks may triple the number of items recalled. Keep practicing in this way until you're satisfied with your improvement.

When learning a series of items or numbers, devote at least several minutes to each practice session.

This type of mental practice is also very effective for retrieving information you once knew well but now recall poorly. If you expect to be called on at a meeting to discuss a topic that is hazy, practice retrieving the topic several times beforehand. Even without any relearning, you'll recall more information and have faster access to it at the meeting if you practice your remembering ahead of time. By combining relearning with remembering practice, you can further improve your performance.

Daily life presents plenty of opportunities to practice for memory tasks. You frequently have occasion to remember names you may know but haven't thought about in a long time, such as one-time movie stars or distant relatives.

Daily life gives you plenty of opportunity to practice mental manipulations.

Other memory tasks don't come up every day. You seldom get to "practice" receiving and remembering directions to a new location, for example. When this situation does come up, it's usually important that you get to the place you want to go, and quickly. Few people trust their recall of verbal directions well enough to do without practice.

If you want to improve your performance of uncommon tasks, you need to devise ways to *simulate* the experience. In the example above, you could practice receiving directions the next time you are a passenger in a car and the *driver* is receiving the directions. If you want to improve your ability to remember names, you might watch talk shows on television and attempt to register the names of guests you don't know.

This *contrived practice* can be done alone or covertly when you are in the company of others. Certain computer software packages now available will take a person through training exercises that teach the use of various memory manipulations.

Even without direct or simulated practice, you can run through memory tasks in your mind. Imagine a memory situation you'd like to conquer. Next, imagine what you would have to do to succeed—using appropriate mental manipulations, taking good care of yourself, adopting a positive view towards the task, making use of the environment when you perform the task, and so on. Athletes report that mentally visualizing a perfect performance helps them focus their approach in actual competition. It can do the same for your memory.

It requires work, but if you really want a superior memory, practicing memory tasks over a considerable period of time is essential. Unfortunately, you can no more expect to improve your memory by merely reading a book than you would your tennis or golf game.

The Game Plan

I know I've been stressing that practice and hard work are keys to developing a good memory. But that doesn't mean you can't have a little fun, too. Another way to practice your memory skills is by playing games.

Just about any board, card, or parlor game challenges you to remember information. Games like Concentration, bridge, gin, pinochle, poker, and crossword puzzles almost can be viewed like memory improvement courses (and are probably more helpful than many of them). Trivial Pursuit relies entirely on memory. Scrabble and Boggle are excellent for reviving fading word skills. Even TV game shows such as "College Bowl" and "Jeopardy" are based on challenging your memory.

Playing games is a fun way of improving your memory skills.

These games will not themselves drastically improve your general memory skills, but regularly playing a variety of them may help you discover some useful memory manipulations of your own. Also, you can use your performance at these games as a "memory thermometer." If you see that your performance dips below the usual level of people you know, it may prompt you to evaluate your memory's condition and take steps to improve it.

Role-Playing

Another good way to practice your memory skills and have fun at the same time is by role-playing. Ask someone you know well and feel comfortable with to help you recreate a memory situation at which you want to improve.

Suppose you want to improve your ability to learn names when introduced to new people. (This situation, in fact, is the memory task most *disliked* by both young and old.) Ask your partner to make up names and pretend to introduce himself or herself as if you were meeting for the first time, such as at a party. These simulated introductions, if practiced thoroughly, will make you better at remembering names during *real* introductions. And if you reverse roles with your partner in this role-play, you'll be able to compare your skill with his or hers. This situation is one example in which practicing by yourself would be useless, but working with another person can truly be helpful—and even fun.

Summary

You can work toward superior memory ability by developing a sense of memory savvy and street smarts. This means not only knowing mental strategies and techniques, but also understanding how, when, and where to use them.

Epilogue

GREAT EXPECTATIONS

The mystery of memory is far too complex to be served by a few time-honored manipulations toward memory improvement. Modern researchers believe in providing a person with many methods which allow for a flexible response to diversify memory tasks. After all, your memory is measured by its ability to respond effectively to your every need, whatever the situation.

Each generation has its memory superstars who do amazing things like memorizing the entire Bible, reading a newspaper and reciting its contents front to back (or vice versa), repeating up to 80 digits in correct order right after they are read once, and recalling the names of thousands of acquaintances. Though these people surely have special memory gifts, their abilities for recall are not based on these gifts alone. Effort and experience, both available to everyone, also play a part. Maybe you aren't capable of stellar feats of memory, but you can certainly achieve substantial improvement in your ability to remember.

Regardless of how humble or lofty your ambitions for improved memory performance might be, the avenue to progress lies in developing a repertoire of various memory manipulations, especially those that are task-specific. It's true: You can remember anything you really want to remember.

I hope this book smoothes your path toward a more effective memory. In the words of an ancient wise man, my wish to you is this:

> *May you always*
> *Remember what is important*
> *And forget the rest.*

To the Reader. . .

As you try the methods recommended in this book, you may come up with fresh techniques of your own that might help other people to achieve a better memory. Such ideas (and your reactions to those presented here) would be extremely valuable to me in my research and in any future revision of this book. Send your comments to: Dr. Douglas Herrmann, 7420 Rosewood Manor Lane, Gaithersburg, MD 20879.

BIBLIOGRAPHY

A great deal of research has been done in the field of memory in recent years and this section lists books, papers, and scientific articles that formed the core of my thinking as I wrote *Supermemory*.

Chapter 1

Harris, J. E., and Morris, P. E. *Everyday Memory and Action and Absent Mindedness.* London: Academic Press, 1984.

Loftus, E. *Memory: Surprising New Insights into How We Remember and Why We Forget.* Reading, Mass.: Addison-Wesley Publishing Company, 1980.

Miller, G. A., Galanter, E., and Pribram, K. H. *Plans and the Structure of Behavior.* New York: Holt, Rinehart, and Winston, 1960.

Norman, D. A. *Learning and Memory.* New York: W. H. Freeman, 1982.

Chapter 2

Atkinson, R. C., and Shiffrin, R. M. "Human Memory: A Proposed System and Its Control Processes." In *The*

Psychology of Learning and Motivation, edited by K. W. Spence and J. T. Spence, vol. 2. New York: Academic Press, 1968.

Bachman, L. "Varieties of Memory Compensation of Older Adults in Episodic Remembering." In *Everyday Cognition in Adult and Late Life,* edited by L. Poon, D. Rubin, and B. Wilson. New York: Cambridge University Press, 1990. In press.

Baddeley, A. D. "Domains of Recollection." *Psychological Review* 89 (1982): 708–729.

Bellezza, F. S. *Improve Your Memory Skills.* Englewood Cliffs, N.J.: Prentice-Hall, 1982.

Craik, F. I. M., and Lockhart, R. S. "Levels of Processing: A Framework for Memory Research." *Journal of Verbal Learning and Verbal Behavior* 11 (1973): 671–684.

Druckman, D., and Swets, J. A. *Enhancing Human Performance.* Washington, D.C.: National Academy Press, 1988.

Gruneberg, M. M., Morris, P. E., and Sykes, R. N., eds. *Practical Aspects of Memory.* London: Academic Press, 1978.

———. *Practical Aspects of Memory.* Chichester: Wiley, 1988.

Harris, J. E., and Wilkins, A. J. "Remembering To Do Things: A Theoretical Framework and an Illustrative Experiment." *Human Learning* 1 (1982): 123–136.

Herrmann, D. J., Rea, A., and Andrzejewski, S. "The Need for a New Approach to Memory Training." In *Practical Aspects of Memory,* edited by M. M. Gruneberg, P. E. Morris, and R. N. Sykes. Chichester: Wiley, 1988.

Herrmann, D. J., and Searleman, A. "A Multi-Modal Approach to Memory." In *Advances in Learning and Motivation,* edited by G. Bower. New York: Academic Press, 1990. In press.

Howe, M., ed. *Adult Learning: Psychological Research and Applications.* London: Wiley and Sons, 1977.

James, W. *The Principles of Psychology.* New York: Henry Holt and Company, 1890.

Landauer, T. K. "How Much Do People Remember? Some Estimates of the Quantity of Learned Information in Long-Term Memory." *Cognitive Science* 10 (1986): 477–494.

McEvoy, C. L., and Moon, J. R. "Assessment and Treatment of Everyday Memory Problems in the Elderly." In *Practical Aspects of Memory,* edited by M. M. Gruneberg, P. E. Morris, and R. N. Sykes. Chichester: Wiley, 1988.

Neisser, U. "Memory: What Are the Important Questions." In *Practical Aspects of Memory,* edited by M. M. Gruneberg, P. E. Morris, and R. N. Sykes. London: Academic Press, 1978.

———. *Memory Observed: Remembering in Natural Contexts.* San Francisco: W. H. Freeman, 1982.

Parks, D., Cavanaugh, J., and Smith, A. "Metamemory[2]: Memory Researchers' Knowledge of Their Own Memory Abilities." American Psychological Association meeting, Washington, D.C., 1986.

Poon, L. W. "A Systems Approach for the Assessment and Treatment of Memory Problems." In *The Comprehensive Handbook of Behavior Medicine*, edited by J. M. Ferguson and C. B. Taylor, vol. 1. Great Neck, N.Y.: PMA Publishing Corporation, 1980.

Simon, H. A. "The Parameters of Human Memory." In *Human Memory and Cognitive Capabilities*, edited by F. Klix and H. Hagendorf. Amsterdam: North Holland Press, 1986.

Talland, G. A. *Disorders of Memory.* Harmonsworth, Middlesex: Penguin, 1968.

Tulving, E. "How Many Memory Systems Are There?" *American Psychologist* 40 (1984): 385–398.

West, R. *Memory Fitness Over 40.* Gainesville, Fla.: Triad Publishing Company, 1985.

Wilson, B. *Rehabilitation of Memory.* New York: Guilford Press, 1987.

Wilson, B., and Moffat, N. *Clinical Management of Memory Problems.* Rockville, Md.: Aspen Systems, 1984.

Yesavage, J. A., Sheikh, J. I., and Lapp, D. "Mnemonics as Modified for Use by the Elderly." In *Everyday Cognition in Adult and Late Life*, edited by L. Poon, D. Rubin, and B. Wilson. New York: Cambridge University Press, 1990.

Chapter 3

Buschke, H. "Criteria for the Identification of Memory Deficits: Implications for the Design of Memory Tests." In *Memory and Learning*, edited by D. Gorfein and R. Hoffman. Hillsdale, N.J.: Lawrence Erlbaum Associates, 1987.

Dixon, R. A., Hertzog, C., and Hultsch, D. F. "The Multiple Relationships among Metamemory in Adulthood (MIA) Scales and Cognitive Abilities in Adulthood." *Human Learning* 5 (1986): 165–178.

Forrest-Pressley, D. L., MacKinnon, G. E., and Waller, T. G. *Metacognition, Cognition, and Human Performance*, vols. 1 and 2. New York: Academic Press, 1985.

Greenwald, A. G. "The Totalitarian Ego." *American Psychologist* 35 (1980): 603–618.

Harris, J. E., and Morris, P. E. *Everyday Memory and Action and Absent Mindedness*. London: Academic Press, 1984.

Herrmann, D. J. "Know Thy Memory: The Use of Questionnaires to Assess and Study Memory." *Psychological Bulletin* 92 (1982): 434–452.

————. "Questionnaires about Memory." In *Everyday Memory and Action and Absent Mindedness*, edited by J. Harris and P. Morris. London: Academic Press, 1984.

Herrmann, D. J., Grubs, L., Sigmundi, R., and Grueneich, R. "Awareness of Memory Ability Before and After Relevant Memory Experience." *Human Learning* 5 (1986): 91–108.

Klatzky, R. L. *Memory and Awareness.* New York: W. H. Freeman, 1984.

Morris, P. "The Cognitive Psychology of Self-Reports." In *Everyday Memory and Action and Absent Mindedness*, edited by J. Harris and P. Morris. London: Academic Press, 1984.

Poon, L. W., ed. *Handbook for Clinical Memory Assessment.* Washington, D.C.: American Psychological Association, 1986.

Reason, J., and MyCielska, M. *Absentmindedness.* Hillsdale, N.J.: Prentice-Hall, 1983.

Shlecter, T. M., and Herrmann, D. J. "Multimethod Approach for Investigating Everyday Memory." Eastern Psychological Association meeting, New York, 1981.

Sternberg, R. J. *Human Abilities.* New York: W. H. Freeman, 1985.

Wechsler, D. "A Standardized Memory Scale for Clinical Use." *Journal of Psychology* 19 (1945): 87–95.

Wilding, J., and Valentine, E. "Searching for Superior Memories." In *Practical Aspects of Memory*, edited by M. M. Gruneberg, P. E. Morris, and R. N. Sykes. Chichester: Wiley, 1988.

Chapter 4

Alzheimer, A. "Uber eine eigenartige Erkranskung der Hirn-rinde." *Allg. Z. Psychiatrie-Gerichtlich Med* 64 (1907): 146–148.

Birnbaum, I., and Parker, E., eds. *Alcohol and Human Memory.* Hillsdale, N.J.: Lawrence Erlbaum Associates, 1977.

Blumenthal, J. A., and Madden, D. J. "Effects of Aerobic Exercise Training, Age, and Physical Fitness on Memory-Search Performance." *Psychology and Aging* 3 (1988): 280–285.

Borkowski, J. G., Carr, M., and Rellinger, E. "Self-Regulated Cognition: Interdependence of Metacognition, Attributions, and Self-Esteem." In *Dimensions of Therapy,* edited by B. Jones. Hillsdale, N.J.: Lawrence Erlbaum Associates, 1987.

Bower, G. H. "Mood and Memory." *American Psychologist* 36 (1981): 129–148.

Broadbent, D. E., Cooper, P. F., Fitzgerald, P., and Parkes, K. R. "The Cognitive Failures Questionnaire (CFQ) and Its Correlates." *British Journal of Psychology* 21 (1982): 1–16.

Cutler, S. J., and Grams, A. E. "Correlates of Self-Reported Everyday Memory Problems." *Journal of Gerontology* 43 (1988): 582–590.

Darley, C. F., et al. "Marijuana and Retrieval from Short-Term Memory." *Psychopharmacologia* 29 (1973): 231–238.

Erdelyi, M. H., and Goldberg, B. "Let's not Sweep Repression under the Rug: Toward a Cognitive Psychology of Repression." In *Functional Disorders of Memory,* edited by J. F. Kihlstrom and F. J. Evans. Hillsdale, N.J.: Lawrence Erlbaum Associates, 1979.

Erikson, G. C., et al. "The Effects of Caffeine on Memory for Word Lists." *Physiology and Behavior* 35 (1985): 47–51.

Folkard, S., and Monk, R. "Time of Day Effects in Immediate and Delayed Memory." In *Practical Aspects of Memory,* edited by M. M. Gruneberg, P. E. Morris, and R. N. Sykes. London: Academic Press, 1978.

Gold, P. E. "Sweet Memories." *American Scientist* 75 (1987): 151–155.

Hodgson, R., and Miller, P. *Self Watching.* London: Century Publishing Company, 1982.

Idzikowski, C. "The Effects of Drugs on Human Memory." In *Practical Aspects of Memory,* edited by M. M. Gruneberg, P. E. Morris, and R. N. Sykes. Chichester: Wiley, 1988.

———. "Sleep and Memory." *British Journal of Psychology* 75 (1984): 439–449.

Khan, A. U. *Clinical Disorders of Memory.* New York: Plenum, 1986.

Kihlstrom, J. F., and Evans, F. J. *Functional Disorders of Memory.* Hillsdale, N.J.: Lawrence Erlbaum Associates, 1979.

Lowe, G. "State-Dependent Retrieval Effects with Social Drugs." In *Practical Aspects of Memory,* edited by M. M. Gruneberg, P. E. Morris, and R. N. Sykes. Chichester: Wiley, 1988.

Matlin, M., and Stang, D. *The Pollyanna Principle.* Cambridge, Mass.: Schenkman, 1978.

Middleton, A. E. *Memory Systems: New and Old.* New York: G. S. Fellows, 1888.

Miles, C., and Smith, A. P. "Combined Effects of Noise and Nightwork on Running Memory." In *Practical Aspects of Memory,* edited by M. M. Gruneberg, P. E. Morris, and R. N. Sykes. Chichester: Wiley, 1988.

Parker, E. S., and Weingartner, H. "Retrograde Facilitations of Human Memory by Drugs." In *Memory Consolidation: Psychology of Cognition,* edited by H. Weingartner and E. S. Parker. Hillsdale: Lawrence Erlbaum Associates, 1985.

Poon, L. W., Rubin, D. C., and Wilson, B. A., eds. *Everyday Cognition in Adult and Late Life (The Fifth Talland Conference).* New York: Cambridge University Press, 1988.

Reason, J. T., and Lucas, D. "Using Cognitive Diaries to Investigate Naturally Occurring Memory Blocks." In *Everyday Memory and Action and Absent Mindedness,* edited by J. Harris and P. Morris. London: Academic Press, 1984.

Reason, J. T., and MyCielska, M. *Absentmindedness.* Hillsdale, N.J.: Prentice-Hall, 1983.

Smith, A. "Effects of Meals on Memory and Attention." In *Practical Aspects of Memory,* edited by M. M. Gruneberg, P. E. Morris, and R. N. Sykes. Chichester: Wiley, 1988.

Spielberger, C. D., Gonzales, H. P., and Fletcher, T. "Test Anxiety Reduction, Learning Strategies, and Academic Performance." In *Cognitive and Affective Learning Strategies,* edited by H. F. O'Neill and C. D. Spielberger. New York: Academic Press, 1979.

Squire, L. *Memory and Brain.* New York: Oxford University Press, 1987.

Squire, L. R., and Butters, N. *Neuropsychology of Memory.* New York: Guilford Press, 1984.

Stollery, B. T. "Neurotoxic Exposure and Memory Function." In *Practical Aspects of Memory,* edited by M. M. Gruneberg, P. E. Morris, and R. N. Sykes. Chichester: Wiley, 1988.

Swanson, J. M., and Kinsbourne, M. "State-Dependent Learning and Retrieval: Methodological Cautions and Theoretical Consideration." In *Functional Disorders of Memory,* edited by J. F. Kihlstrom and F. J. Evans. Hillsdale, N.J.: Lawrence Erlbaum Associates, 1979.

Watts, F. N. "Memory Deficit in Depression." In *Practical Aspects of Memory,* edited by M. M. Gruneberg, P. E. Morris, and R. N. Sykes. Chichester: Wiley, 1988.

Wilson, B. A. *The Rehabilitation of Memory.* New York: Guilford Press, 1987.

Wilson, B. A., and Moffat, N. *Clinical Management of Memory Problems.* Rockville, Md.: Aspen Systems, 1984.

Wyon, D. P., Andersen, B., and Lundqvist, G. R. "The Effects of Moderate Heat Stress on Mental Performance." *Scandinavian Journal of Work Environment and Health* 5 (1979): 352–361.

Yesavage, J. A., and Rolf, J. "Effects of Relaxation and Mnemonics on Memory, Attention, and Anxiety in the Elderly." *Experimental Aging Research* 10 (1984): 211–214.

Chapter 5

Ash, S. E. "Studies of Independence and Conformity: A Minority of One Against a Unanimous Majority." *Psychological Monographs* 70, 9, whole no. 416 (1956).

Crawford, M., et al. "Gender Differences in the Perception of Memory Abilities in Others." *British Journal of Psychology* 80 (1989): 391–401.

Gentry, M., and Herrmann, D. J. "Memory Contrivances in Everyday Life." *Personality and Social Psychology Bulletin,* 1990.

Goldsmith, L. R., and Pillemer, D. B. "Memories of Statements Spoken in Everyday Context." *Applied Cognitive Psychology* 2 (1988): 273–286.

Graumann, C. F. "Memorabilia, Mementos, Memoranda: Toward an Ecology of Memory." In *Human Memory and Cognitive Capabilities, Part A,* edited by F. Klix and H. Hagendorf. Amsterdam: North Holland Press, 1985.

Greenwald, A. G. "The Totalitarian Ego." *American Psychologist* 35 (1980): 603–618.

Hamlett, K. W., Best, D. L., and Davis, S. W. "Modification of Memory Complaint and Memory Performance in Elderly Adults." Unpublished manuscript. Washington, D.C.: Catholic University of America, 1985.

Hastie, R., et al. *Person Memory.* Hillsdale, N.J.: Lawrence Erlbaum Associates, 1980.

Neisser, U. "Time Present and Time Past." In *Practical Aspects of Memory,* edited by M. M. Gruneberg, P. E. Morris, and R. N. Sykes. Chichester: Wiley, 1988.

Searle, J. R. *Speech Acts.* New York: Cambridge University Press, 1969.

Chapter 6

Adams, L. T. "Improving Memory: Can Retrieval Strategies Help?" *Human Learning* 4 (1985): 281–297.

Anderson, J. R. *The Architecture of Cognition.* Cambridge, Mass.: Harvard University Press, 1983.

———. "Acquisition of a Cognitive Skill." *Psychological Review* 89 (1982): 396–406.

Bellezza, F. S. *Improving Your Memory Skills.* Englewood Cliffs, N.J.: Prentice-Hall, 1982.

————. "Mnemonic Devices: Classification, Characteristics, and Criteria." *Review of Educational Research* 51 (1981): 247–275.

————. "Mnemonic-Device Instruction with Adults." In *Cognitive Strategy Research,* edited by M. Pressley and J. R. Levin. New York: Springer-Verlag, 1983.

Chase, W. G., and Ericsson, K. A. "Skill and Working Memory." In *The Psychology of Learning and Motivation,* edited by G. H. Bower, vol. 16. New York: Academic Press, 1982.

Cohen, G. *Memory in the Real World.* Hillsdale, N.J.: Lawrence Erlbaum Associates, 1980.

Dorner, D. "Intention Memory and Intention Regulation." In *Human Memory and Cognitive Capabilities,* edited by F. Klix and H. Hagendorf. Amsterdam: North Holland Press, 1987.

Ericsson, K. A. "Memory Skill." *Canadian Journal of Psychology* 39 (1985): 188–231.

Feinaigle, M. G. von. *The New Art of Memory.* London: Sherwood, Neely, and Jones Press, 1812.

Geiselman, R. E., et al. "Enhancement of Eyewitness Memory with the Cognitive Interview." *American Journal of Psychology* 99 (1986): 385–401.

Herrmann, D. J., Buschke, H., and Gall, M. "Improving Retrieval." *Applied Cognitive Psychology* 9 (1986): 27–33.

Herrmann, D. J., Rea, A., and Andrzejewski, S. "The Need for a New Approach to Memory Training." In *Practical Aspects of Memory*, edited by M. M. Gruneberg, P. E. Morris, and R. N. Sykes. Chichester: Wiley, 1988.

Higbee, K. L. "What Do College Students Get from a Memory Improvement Course." Eastern Psychological Association, New York City, 1981.

————. *Your Memory.* 2d ed. Englewood Cliffs, N.J.: Prentice-Hall, 1988.

Kolodner, J. L. *Retrieval and Organizational Strategies in Conceptual Memory: A Computer Model.* Hillsdale, N.J.: Lawrence Erlbaum Associates, 1984.

Lapp, D. "Commitment: Essential Ingredient in Memory Training." *Clinical Gerontologist* 2 (1983): 58–60.

McDaniel, M. A., and Pressley, M. *Imagery and Related Mnemonic Processes: Theories, Individual Differences, and Applications.* New York: Springer-Verlag, 1987.

Morris, P. E. "Practical Strategies for Human Learning and Remembering." In *Adult Learning: Psychological Research and Applications*, edited by M. Howe. London: Wiley and Sons, 1977.

Neisser, U., and Winograd, E. *Remembering Reconsidered.* New York: Cambridge University Press, 1988.

Parks, D., Cavanaugh, J., and Smith, A. "Metamemory[2]: Memory Researchers' Knowledge of Their Own Memory Abilities." American Psychological Association meeting, Washington, D.C., 1986.

Pressley, M., and Levin, J. R. *Cognitive Strategy Research.* New York: Springer-Verlag, 1983.

Pugh, E. *A Dictionary of Acronyms and Abbreviations.* London: Anchor Books, 1970.

Rubin, D. C. *Autobiographical Memory.* New York: Cambridge University Press, 1986.

Schank, R. C. *Dynamic Memory.* New York: Cambridge University Press, 1982.

Schooler, J. W., Gerhard, D., and Loftus, E. "Qualities of the Unreal." *Journal of Experimental Psychology: Learning, Memory, and Cognition* 12 (1986): 171–181.

Segal, J. W., Chipman, S. F., and Glaser, R., eds. *Thinking and Learning Skills*, vols. 1 and 2. Hillsdale, N.J.: Lawrence Erlbaum Associates, 1985.

Simon, H. A., and Gilmarten, K. "A Simulation of Memory for Chess Positions." *Cognitive Psychology* 5 (1973): 29–46.

White, D. R. *A Glossary of Acronyms, Abbreviations and Symbols.* Germantown, Md.: Don White Consultants, 1971.

Young, M. N. *Bibliography of Memory.* Philadelphia: Chilton, 1961.

Young, M. N., and Gibson, W. B. *How to Develop an Exceptional Memory.* Hollywood: Wilshire Books, 1962.

Chapter 7

Beach, K. "Learning to Become a Bartender: The Role of External Memory Cues at Work." Eastern Psychological Association meeting, Boston, 1985.

Cavanaugh, J. C., Grady, J. G., and Perlmutter, M. "Forgetting and Use of Memory Aids in 20- to 70-Year-Olds' Everyday Life." *International Journal of Aging and Human Development* 17 (1983): 113–122.

Estes, W. K. "Is Human Memory Obsolete?" *American Scientist* 68 (1980): 62–68.

Harris, J. E. "Methods of Improving Memory." In *Clinical Management of Memory Problems*, edited by B. A. Wilson and N. Moffatt. Beckenham: Croom Helm, 1984.

Harris, J. E., and Wilkins, A. J. "Remembering To Do Things: A Theoretical Framework and an Illustrative Experiment." *Human Learning* 1 (1982): 123–136.

Herrmann, D. J., and Petro, S. "Commercial Memory Aids." *Applied Cognitive Psychology*, 1990. In press.

Hertel, P. "External Memory." In *Practical Aspects of Memory*, edited by M. M. Gruneberg, P. E. Morris, and R. N. Sykes. Chichester: Wiley, 1988.

Malone, T. W. "How Do People Organize Their Desks? Implications for the Design of Office Information Systems." *ACM Transactions on Office Information Systems* 1 (1983): 99–112.

Parks, D., Cavanaugh, J., and Smith, A. "Metamemory[2]: Memory Researchers' Knowledge of Their Own Memory Abilities." American Psychological Association meeting, Washington, D.C., 1986.

Winograd, E., and Soloway, R. M. "Hiding Things from Ourselves: Objects and Special Places." *Journal of Experimental Psychology: General* 115 (1985): 366–372.

Yates, F. *The Arts of Memory.* Chicago: Chicago University Press, 1966.

Chapter 8

Baddeley, A. D. "Domains of Recollection." *Psychological Review* 89 (1982): 708–729.

Baltes, P. B., and Kliegel, R. "On the Dynamics between Growth and Decline in the Aging of Intelligence and Memory." In *Proceedings of the Thirteenth World Conference of Neurology,* edited by K. Poeck. Heidelberg, FR Germany: Springer-Verlag, 1986.

Barclay, C. R., and Subramaniam, G. "Autobiographical Memories and Self-Schemata." *Applied Cognitive Psychology* 1 (1988): 169–182.

Bransford, J. D., and Stein, B. *The Ideal Problem Solver.* New York: W. H. Freeman, 1984.

Chase, W. G., and Ericsson, K. A. "Skill and Working Memory." In *The Psychology of Learning and Motivation,* edited by G. H. Bower, vol. 16. New York: Academic Press, 1982.

Cole, M., and Scribner, S. *Culture and Thought.* New York: Wiley, 1974.

Davies, G. M., and Thomson, D. M. *Memory in Context: Context in Memory.* Chichester: Wiley, 1988.

Ericsson, K. A. "Memory Skill." *Canadian Journal of Psychology* 39 (1985): 188–231.

Gagne, R. M., and Paradise, N. E. "Abilities and Learning Sets in Knowledge Acquisition." *Psychological Monographs* 75, no. 14, whole no. 518 (1961).

Garfunkel, F., and Landau, G. *A Memory Retention Course for the Aged: Guide for Leaders.* Washington, D.C.: The National Council on the Aging, 1981.

Greeno, J. G. "A Perspective on Thinking." *American Psychologist* 44 (1989): 134–141.

Gruneberg, M. M., and Morris, P. E. *Applied Problems in Memory.* New York: Academic Press, 1979.

Gruneberg, M. M., Morris, P. E., and Sykes, R. N. *Practical Aspects of Memory.* London: Academic Press, 1978.

Harlow, H. F. "The Formation of Learning Sets." *Psychological Review* 56 (1949): 51–65.

Harris, J. E., and Morris, P. E. *Everyday Memory and Action and Absent Mindedness.* London: Academic Press, 1984.

Herrmann, D. J. "Task Appropriateness of Mnemonic Techniques." *Perceptual and Motor Skills* 64 (1987): 171–178.

Herrmann, D., Rea, A., and Andrzejewski, S. "The Need for a New Approach to Memory Training." In *Practical Aspects of Memory*, edited by M. M. Gruneberg, P. E. Morris, and R. N. Sykes. Chichester: Wiley, 1988.

Lave, J. *Cognition in Practice.* Cambridge, England: Cambridge University Press, 1989.

Miller, G. A., Galanter, E., and Pribram, K. H. *Plans and the Structure of Behavior.* New York: Holt, Rinehart, and Winston, 1960.

Neisser, U. *Memory Observed.* New York: W. H. Freeman, 1982.

Rybash, J. M., Hoyer, W. J., and Roodin, P. A. *Adult Cognition and Aging.* New York: Pergamon, 1986.

Schank, R. C. *Dynamic Memory.* Cambridge, England: Cambridge University Press, 1982.

Schooler, J. W., and Schooler, T. E. "Verbal Overshadowing of Visual Memories: Some Things Are Better Left Unsaid." *Cognitive Psychology,* 1990. In press.

Simon, H. A., and Gilmarten, K. "A Simulation of Memory for Chess Positions." *Cognitive Psychology* 5 (1973): 29–46.

Stern, L., and Fogler, J. *Improving Your Memory: A Guide for Older Adults.* Ann Arbor, Mich.: Turner Geriatric Services, University of Michigan Medical Center, 1989.

Thorndike, E. L. "Mental Discipline in High School Studies." *Journal of Educational Psychology* 15 (1924): 1–22, 83–98.

Young, M. N. *Bibliography of Memory.* Philadelphia: Chilton, 1961.

Chapter 9

Baltes, P. B., and Kliegel, R. "On the Dynamics between Growth and Decline in the Aging of Intelligence and Memory." In *Proceedings of the Thirteenth World Conference of Neurology,* edited by K. Poeck. Heidelberg, FR Germany: Springer-Verlag, 1986.

Bellezza, F. S., and Buck, D. K. "Expert Knowledge as Mnemonic Cues." *Applied Cognitive Psychology* 2 (1988): 147–162.

Breme, F. J., and Rosen, D. A. "How to Flunk Out: A Paradoxical Approach to Study Skills." ERIC Reports, ED 240 478, 1982.

Chase, W. G., and Ericsson, K. A. "Skill and Working Memory." In *The Psychology of Learning and Motivation,* edited by G. H. Bower, vol. 16. New York: Academic Press, 1982.

Golick, M. *Learning through Card Games.* Exeter: A. Wheaton, 1973.

Hardy, L., and Ringland, A. "Mental Training and the Inner Game." *Human Learning* 3 (1984): 143–226.

Herrmann, D. J., Buschke, H., and Gall, M. "Improving Retrieval." *Applied Cognitive Psychology* 1 (1987): 27–33.

Hodgson, R., and Miller, P. *Self Watching.* London: Century Publishing Company, 1982.

Johnson, M. K., and Raye, C. L. "Reality Monitoring." *Psychological Review* 88 (1981): 67–85.

Morehead, H., and Mott-Smith, G. *Hoyle's Rules of Games.* New York: New American Library, 1946.

Reason, J. T., and MyCielska, M. *Absentmindedness.* Hillsdale, N.J.: Prentice-Hall, 1983.

Schneider, W., and Shiffrin, R. M. "Controlled and Automatic Human Information Processing: I. Detection, Search, and Attention." *Psychological Review* 84 (1977): 1–66.

————. "Controlled and Automatic Human Information Processing: II. Perceptual Learning, Automatic Attending, and a General Theory." *Psychological Review* 84 (1977): 127–190.

Epilogue

Atkinson, W. W. *Memory: How to Develop, Train and Use It.* Holyoke, Mass.: Elizabeth Towne, 1912.

Brown, E., and Deffenbacher, K. "Forgotten Mnemonists." *Journal of the History of the Behavioral Sciences* 11 (1975): 342–349.

Herrmann, D. J., and Chaffin, R. *Memory in Historical Perspective.* New York: Springer-Verlag, 1988.

Hunt, E., and Love, T. "How Good Can Memory Be?" In *Coding Processes in Human Memory*, edited by A. W. Melton and E. Martin. Washington, D.C.: V. H. Winston and Sons, 1972.

Neisser, U. *Memory Observed*. New York: W. H. Freeman, 1982.

INDEX